GREECE

IN COLOUR

EDITIONS   G.   GOUVOUSSIS

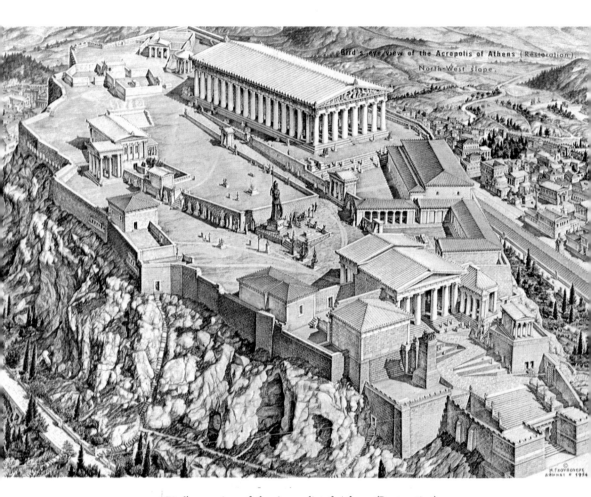

Bird's eye view of the Acropolis of Athens (Restoration).

CONTENTS

PREFACE

'Hostile to the church, friendly to Jesus Christ.' These words describe large numbers of people, especially young people, today.

They are opposed to anything which savours of institutionalism. They detest the establishment and its entrenched privileges. And they reject the church – not without some justification – because they regard it as impossibly corrupted by such evils.

Yet what they have rejected is the contemporary church, not Jesus Christ himself. It is precisely because they see a contradiction between the founder of Christianity and the current state of the church he founded that they are so critical and aloof. The person and teaching of Jesus have not lost their appeal, however. For one thing, he was himself an anti-establishment figure, and some of his words had revolutionary overtones. His ideals appear to have been incorruptible. He breathed love and peace wherever he went. And, for another thing, he invariably practised what he preached.

But was he *true*?

An appreciable number of people throughout the world are still brought up in Christian homes in which the truth of Christ and of Christianity is assumed. But when their critical faculties develop and they begin to think for themselves, they find it easier to discard the religion of their childhood than make the effort to investigate its credentials.

Very many others do not grow up in a Christian environment. Instead they absorb the teaching of Hinduism, Buddhism or

Islam, or the ethos of secular humanism, communism or existentialism.

Yet both groups, if and when they read about Jesus, find that he holds for them a fascination they cannot easily escape.

So our starting-point is the historical figure of Jesus of Nazareth. He certainly existed. There is no reasonable doubt about that. His historicity is vouched for by pagan as well as Christian writers.

He was also very much a human being, whatever else may be said about him. He was born, he grew, he worked and sweated, rested and slept, he ate and drank, suffered and died like other men. He had a real human body and real human emotions.

But can we really believe that he was also in some sense 'God'? Is not the deity of Jesus a rather picturesque Christian superstition? Is there any evidence for the amazing Christian assertion that the carpenter of Nazareth was the unique Son of God?

This question is fundamental. We cannot dodge it. We must be honest. If Jesus was not God in human flesh, Christianity is exploded. We are left with just another religion with some beautiful ideas and noble ethics; its unique distinction has gone.

But there *is* evidence for the deity of Jesus – good, strong, historical, cumulative evidence; evidence to which an honest person can subscribe without committing intellectual suicide. There are the extravagant claims which Jesus made for himself, so bold and yet so unassuming. Then there is his incomparable character. His strength and gentleness, his uncompromising righteousness and tender compassion, his care for children and his love for outcasts, his self-mastery and self-sacrifice have won the admiration of the world. What is more, his cruel death was not the end of him. It is claimed that he rose again from death, and the circumstantial evidence for his resurrection is most compelling.

Supposing Jesus was the Son of God, is basic Christianity merely an acceptance of this fact? No. Once persuaded of the deity of his person, we must examine the nature of his work. What did he come to do? The biblical answer is, he 'came into the world to save sinners'. Jesus of Nazareth is the heaven-sent Saviour we sinners need. We need to be forgiven and restored to fellowship with the all-holy God, from whom our sins have separated us. We need to be set free from our selfishness and given strength to live up to our ideals. We need to learn to love one another, friend and foe alike. This is the meaning of 'salvation'. This is what Christ came to win for us by his death and resurrection.

Then is basic Christianity the belief that Jesus is the Son of God who came to be the Saviour of the world? No, it is not even that. To assent to his divine person, to acknowledge man's need of salvation, and to believe in Christ's saving work are not enough. Christianity is not just a creed; it involves action. Our intellectual belief may be beyond criticism; but we have to translate our beliefs into deeds.

What must we do, then? We must commit ourselves, heart and mind, soul and will, home and life, personally and un-reservedly to Jesus Christ. We must humble ourselves before him. We must trust in him as *our* Saviour and submit to him as *our* Lord; and then go on to take our place as loyal members of the church and responsible citizens in the community.

Such is basic Christianity, and the theme of this book. But before we come to the evidence for Jesus Christ's deity, an introductory chapter on the right approach is necessary. The Christian claim is that we can find God in Jesus Christ. It should be a help to us in examining this claim if we realize both that God is himself seeking us and that we must ourselves seek God.

1 THE RIGHT APPROACH

'In the beginning God.' The first four words of the Bible are more than an introduction to the creation story or to the book of Genesis. They supply the key which opens our understanding to the Bible as a whole. They tell us that the religion of the Bible is a religion of the initiative of God.

You can never take God by surprise. You can never anticipate him. He always makes the first move. He is always there 'in the beginning'. Before man existed, God acted. Before man stirs himself to seek God, God has sought man. In the Bible we do not see man groping after God; we see God reaching after man.

Many people visualize a God who sits comfortably on a distant throne, remote, aloof, uninterested, and indifferent to the needs of mortals, until, it may be, they can badger him into taking action on their behalf. Such a view is wholly false. The Bible reveals a God who, long before it even occurs to man to turn to him, while man is still lost in darkness and sunk in sin, takes the initiative, rises from his throne, lays aside his glory, and stoops to seek until he finds him.

This sovereign, anticipating activity of God is seen in many ways. He has taken the initiative in *creation*, bringing the universe and its contents into existence: 'In the beginning God created the heavens and the earth.' He has taken the initiative in *revelation*, making known to mankind both his nature and his will: 'In many and various ways God spoke of old to our fathers by the prophets; but in these last days he has spoken to us by a Son ... ' He has taken the initiative in *salvation*, coming in Jesus Christ to set men and women free from their sins: 'God . . . has visited and redeemed his people.'[1]

God has created. God has spoken. God has acted. These statements of God's initiative in three different spheres form a summary of the religion of the Bible. It is with the second and third that we shall be concerned in this book, because basic Christianity by definition begins with the historical figure of Jesus Christ. If God has spoken, his last and greatest word to the world is Jesus Christ. If God has acted, his noblest act is the redemption of the world through Jesus Christ.

God has spoken and acted in Jesus Christ. He has said something. He has done something. This means that Christianity is not just pious talk. It is neither a collection of religious ideas nor a catalogue of rules. It is a 'gospel' (*i.e.* good news) – in Paul's words 'the gospel of God . . . concerning his Son . . . Jesus Christ our Lord'.[2] It is not primarily an invitation to man to do anything; it is supremely a declaration of what God has done in Christ for human beings like ourselves.

God has spoken

Man is an insatiably inquisitive creature. His mind is so made that it cannot rest. It is always prying into the unknown. He pursues knowledge with restless energy. His life is a voyage of discovery. He is always questing, exploring, investigating, researching. He never grows out of the child's interminable 'Why?'

When man's mind begins to concern itself with God, however, it is baffled. It gropes in the dark. It flounders helplessly out of its depth. Nor is this surprising, because God, whatever or whoever he may be, is infinite, while we are finite creatures. He is altogether beyond our comprehension. Therefore our minds, though wonderfully effective instruments in the empirical sciences, cannot immediately help us here. They

[1] Genesis 1:1; Hebrews 1:1, 2; Luke 1:68.
[2] Romans 1:1-4.

cannot climb up into the infinite mind of God. There is no ladder, only a vast, unmeasured gulf. 'Can you find out the deep things of God?' Job was asked. It is impossible.

And so the situation would have remained if God had not taken the initiative to remedy it. Man would have remained for ever agnostic, asking indeed with Pontius Pilate, 'What is truth?' but never staying for an answer, because never daring to hope that he would receive one. He would be a worshipper, for such is his nature; but all his altars would be inscribed, like the one in Athens, 'To an unknown god'.

But God has spoken. He has taken the initiative to disclose himself. The Christian doctrine of revelation is essentially reasonable. God has 'unveiled' to our minds what would otherwise have been hidden from them. Part of his revelation is in nature:

> 'The heavens are telling the glory of God;
> and the firmament proclaims his handiwork.'

> 'What can be known about God is plain to them (that is, men), because God has shown it to them. Ever since the creation of the world his invisible nature, namely, his eternal power and deity, has been clearly perceived in the things that have been made.'[3]

This is commonly called God's 'general' revelation (because it is made to all men everywhere) or 'natural' revelation (because it is in nature). But this is not enough. It certainly makes known his existence, and something of his divine power, glory and faithfulness. But if man is to come to know God personally, to have his sins forgiven and to enter into relationship with God, he needs a more extensive and practical revelation still. God's self-disclosure must include his holiness, his love and his power to save from sin. This too God has been pleased to give. It is a 'special' revelation, because it was made to a special people (Israel) through special messengers (prophets in the Old Testament and apostles in the New).

It is also 'supernatural', because it was given through a process commonly called 'inspiration', and it found its chief expression in the person and work of Jesus.

[3] Psalm 19:1; Romans 1:19, 20.

13

The way in which the Bible explains and describes this revelation is to say that God has 'spoken'. We ourselves communicate with one another most easily by speech. It is by our words that we disclose what is in our minds. This is even more true of God who has desired to reveal his infinite mind to our finite minds. Since, as the prophet Isaiah put it, his thoughts are as much higher than our thoughts as the heavens are higher than the earth, we could never have come to know them unless he had clothed them in words. So 'the word of the Lord came' to many prophets, until at last Jesus Christ came, and 'the Word became flesh and dwelt among us'.[4]

Similarly, Paul wrote to the Corinthian church, ' . . . since, in the wisdom of God, the world did not know God through wisdom, it pleased God through the folly of what we preach to save those who believe'. Man comes to know God not through his own wisdom but through God's word ('what we preach'), not through human reason but through divine revelation. It is because God has made himself known in Christ that the Christian can boldly go to the agnostic and the superstitious and say to them, as Paul did to the Athenians on the Areopagus, 'What therefore you worship as unknown, this I proclaim to you'.

Much of the controversy between science and religion has arisen through a failure to appreciate this point. The empirical method is largely inappropriate in the sphere of religion. Scientific knowledge advances through observation and experiment. It works on data supplied by the five physical senses. But when we enquire into the metaphysical, no data are immediately available. God today is neither tangible, visible nor audible. Yet there was a time when he chose to speak, and to clothe himself with a body which could be seen and touched. So John began his first Epistle with the claim, 'That which was from the beginning, which we have heard, which we have seen with our eyes, which we have looked upon and touched with our hands . . . we proclaim also to you . . . '

[4] John 1:1, 14.

God has acted

The Christian good news is not confined to a declaration that God has spoken. It also affirms that God has acted.

God has taken the initiative in both these ways because of the character of man's need. For we are not only ignorant; we are sinful. It is not sufficient therefore that God should have revealed himself to us to dispel our ignorance. He must also take action to save us from our sins. He began in Old Testament days. He called Abraham from Ur, making of him and his descendants a nation, delivering them from slavery in Egypt, entering into a covenant with them at Mount Sinai, leading them across the desert into the promised land, guiding and teaching them as his special people.

But all this was a preparation for his greater deed of redemption in Christ. Men needed to be delivered, not from slavery in Egypt or from exile in Babylon, but from the exile and the slavery of sin. It was for this principally that Jesus Christ came. He came as a Saviour.

'. . . You shall call his name Jesus, for he will save his people from their sins.'

'The saying is sure and worthy of full acceptance, that Christ Jesus came into the world to save sinners.'

'For the Son of man came to seek and to save the lost.'

He was like the shepherd who missed the only sheep which was lost from the flock and went out to search until he found it.[5]

Christianity is a religion of salvation, and there is nothing in the non-Christian religions to compare with this message of a God who loved, and came after, and died for, a world of lost sinners.

Man's response

God has spoken. God has acted. The record and interpretation of these divine words and deeds is to be found in the Bible. And there for many people they remain. As far as they are con-

[5] Matthew 1:21; 1 Timothy 1:15; Luke 19:10; Luke 15:3-7.

cerned, what God has said and done belongs to past history; it has not yet come out of history into experience, out of the Bible into life. God has spoken; but have we listened to his word? God has acted; but have we benefited from what he has done?

What we must do will be explained in the rest of this book. At this stage it is necessary to make only one point: we must seek. God has sought us. He is still seeking us. We must seek him. Indeed, God's chief quarrel with man is that he does not seek.

> 'The Lord looks down from heaven
>   upon the children of men,
>   to see if there are any that act wisely,
>   that seek after God.
> They have all gone astray, they are all
>   alike corrupt;
>   there is none that does good,
>   no, not one.'[6]

Yet Jesus promised: 'Seek and you will find'. If we do not seek, we shall never find. The shepherd searched until he found the lost sheep. The woman searched until she found her lost coin. Why should we expect to do less? God desires to be found, but only by those who seek him.

We must seek *diligently*. 'Man is as lazy as he dares to be,' wrote Emerson. But this matter is so serious that we must overcome our natural laziness and apathy and give our minds to the quest. God has little patience with triflers; 'he rewards those who seek him'.[7]

We must seek *humbly*. If apathy is a hindrance to some, pride is an even greater and commoner hindrance to others. We must acknowledge that our minds, being finite, are incapable of discovering God by their own effort without his self-revelation. I am not saying that we should suspend rational thinking. On the contrary, we are told by the psalmist not to be like a horse or a mule which have no understanding. We

[6] Psalm 14:2, 3.
[7] Hebrews 11:6.

16

must use our mind; but we must also admit its limitation. Jesus said,

> 'I thank thee, Father, Lord of heaven and earth, that thou hast hidden these things from the wise and understanding and revealed them to babes.'

It is one of the reasons why Jesus loved children. They are teachable. They are not proud, self-important and critical. We need the open, humble and receptive mind of a little child.

We must seek *honestly*. We must come to what claims to be God's self-revelation not only without pride, but without prejudice; not only with a humble mind, but with an open mind. Every student knows the dangers of approaching his subject with preconceived ideas. Yet many enquirers come to the Bible with their minds already made up. But God's promise is addressed only to the earnest seeker: 'You will seek me and find me; when you seek me with all your heart.'[8] So we must lay aside our prejudice and open our minds to the possibility that Christianity may after all be true.

We must seek *obediently*. This is the hardest condition of all to fulfil. In seeking God we have to be prepared not only to revise our ideas but to reform our lives. The Christian message has a moral challenge. If the message is true, the moral challenge has to be accepted. So God is not a fit object for man's detached scrutiny. You cannot fix God at the end of a telescope or a microscope and say 'How interesting!' God is not interesting. He is deeply upsetting. The same is true of Jesus Christ.

> 'We had thought intellectually to examine him; we find he is spiritually examining us. The rôles are reversed between us. . . . We study Aristotle and are intellectually edified thereby; we study Jesus and are, in the profoundest way, spiritually disturbed. . . . We are constrained to take up some inward moral attitude of heart and will in relation to this Jesus. . . . A man may study Jesus with intellectual impartiality, he cannot do it with moral neutrality. . . . We must declare our colours. To this has our unevasive contact with Jesus

8 Jeremiah 29:13.

brought us. We began it in the calm of the study; we are called out to the field of moral decision.'[9]

This is what Jesus meant when, addressing some unbelieving Jews, he said, 'If any man's will is to do his (that is, God's) will, he shall know whether the teaching is from God or whether I am speaking on my own authority.' The promise is clear: we can know whether Jesus Christ was true or false, whether his teaching was human or divine. But the promise rests on a moral condition. We have to be ready not just to believe, but to obey. We must be prepared to do God's will when he makes it known.

I remember a young man coming to see me when he had just left school and begun work in London. He had given up going to church, he said, because he could not say the Creed without being a hypocrite. He no longer believed it. When he had finished his explanations, I said to him, 'If I were to answer your problems to your complete intellectual satisfaction, would you be willing to alter your manner of life?' He smiled slightly and blushed. His real problem was not intellectual but moral.

This, then, is the spirit in which our search must be conducted. We must cast aside apathy, pride, prejudice and sin, and seek God in scorn of the consequences. Of all these hindrances to effective search the last two are the hardest to overcome, intellectual prejudice and moral self-will. Both are expressions of fear, and fear is the greatest enemy of the truth. Fear paralyses our search. We know that to find God and to accept Jesus Christ would be a very inconvenient experience. It would involve the rethinking of our whole outlook on life and the readjustment of our whole manner of life. And it is a combination of intellectual and moral cowardice which makes us hesitate. We do not find because we do not seek. We do not seek because we do not want to find, and we know that the way to be certain of not finding is not to seek.

[9] P. Carnegie Simpson, *The Fact of Christ*, 1930; James Clarke edition, 1952, pp. 23, 24.

So be open to the possibility that you may be wrong. Christ may in fact be true. And if you want to be a humble, honest, obedient seeker after God, come to the book which claims to be his revelation. Come particularly to the Gospels which tell the story of Jesus Christ. Give him a chance to confront you with himself and to authenticate himself to you. Come with the full consent of your mind and will, ready to believe and obey if God brings conviction to you. Why not read through the Gospel of Mark, or John? You could read either through at a sitting (preferably in a modern translation), to let it make its total impact on you. Then you could re-read it slowly, a chapter a day. Before you read, pray – perhaps something like this:

> 'God, if you exist (and I don't know if you do), and if you can hear this prayer (and I don't know if you can), I want to tell you that I am an honest seeker after the truth. Show me if Jesus is your Son and the Saviour of the world. And if you bring conviction to my mind, I will trust him as my Saviour and follow him as my Lord.'

No-one can pray such a prayer and be disappointed. God is no man's debtor. He honours all earnest search. He rewards all honest seekers. Christ's promise is plain: 'Seek and you will find.'

Part One: Christ's Person

2 THE CLAIMS OF CHRIST

We have seen that it is necessary to seek if we are ever to find. But where shall we begin our search? The Christian answers that the only place at which to begin is the historic person of Jesus of Nazareth; for if God has spoken and acted, it is fully and finally in Jesus Christ that he has done so. The crucial issue is this: was the carpenter of Nazareth the Son of God?

There are two principal reasons why our enquiry into Christianity should begin with the person of Christ. The first is that essentially Christianity is Christ. The person and work of Christ are the rock upon which the Christian religion is built. If he is not who he said he was, and if he did not do what he said he had come to do, the foundation is undermined and the whole superstructure will collapse. Take Christ from Christianity, and you disembowel it; there is practically nothing left. Christ is the centre of Christianity; all else is circumference. We are not concerned primarily to discuss the nature of his philosophy, the value of his system, or the quality of his ethic. Our concern is fundamentally with the character of his person. Who was he?

Second, if Jesus Christ can be shown to have been a uniquely divine person, many other problems begin naturally to be solved. The existence of God is proved and the character of God revealed if Jesus was divine. Again questions about man's duty and destiny, life after death, the purpose and authority of the Old Testament and the meaning of the cross begin to be answered because Jesus taught about these things, and his teaching must be true if his person is divine.

Our investigation must therefore begin with Jesus Christ, and to study him we must turn to the Gospels. It is not necessary at this point to accept them as part of the inspired Scriptures; it will be enough to treat them as the historical documents they undoubtedly are. We cannot here consider the question of their literary origin.[1] It is enough to emphasize that their authors were all Christian men, that Christian men are honest men, and that their contents appear to be both objective and the impressions of eye-witnesses. However, for the time being we shall regard them simply as a substantially accurate record of the life and teaching of Jesus. In doing so, we shall not base our case on a few obscure and isolated proof texts. We shall concentrate on what is general and plain.

Our purpose is to marshal the evidence to prove that Jesus was the Son of God. We shall not be satisfied with a verdict declaring his vague divinity; it is his deity which we mean to establish. We believe him to possess an eternal and essential relation to God possessed by no other person. We regard him neither as God in human disguise, nor as a man with divine qualities, but as the God-man. We are persuaded that Jesus was a historic person possessing two distinct and perfect natures, Godhead and manhood, and in this to be absolutely and for ever unique. Only so could he be worthy not just of our admiration but of our worship.

The evidence is at least threefold. It concerns the claims he made, the character he displayed and his resurrection from the dead. No one argument is conclusive. But the three converging lines point unfalteringly to the same conclusion.

The first witness, then, is that of Christ's own claims. In the words of Archbishop William Temple, 'It is now recognized that the one Christ for whose existence there is any evidence at all is a miraculous Figure making stupendous claims.' It is true that claims do not in themselves constitute evidence, but here is a phenomenon which demands an ex-

[1] For a discussion of the authenticity of the New Testament see F. F. Bruce, *The New Testament Documents*, Inter-Varsity Press, 5th edition, 1960.

planation. For the sake of clarity we shall distinguish between four different kinds of claim.

His self-centred teaching

The most striking feature of the teaching of Jesus is that he was constantly talking about himself. It is true that he spoke much about the fatherhood of God and the kingdom of God. But then he added that he was the Father's 'Son', and that he had come to inaugurate the kingdom. Entry into the kingdom depended on men's response to him. He even did not hesitate to call the kingdom of God 'my kingdom'.

This self-centredness of the teaching of Jesus immediately sets him apart from the other great religious teachers of the world. They were self-effacing. He was self-advancing. They pointed men away from themselves, saying, 'That is the truth, so far as I perceive it; follow that.' Jesus said, 'I am the truth; follow me.' The founder of none of the ethnic religions ever dared to say such a thing. The personal pronoun forces itself repeatedly on our attention as we read his words. For example:

'I am the bread of life; he who comes to me shall not hunger, and he who believes in me shall never thirst.'

'I am the light of the world; he who follows me will not walk in darkness, but will have the light of life.'

'I am the resurrection and the life; he who believes in me, though he die, yet shall he live, and whoever lives and believes in me shall never die.'

'I am the way, and the truth, and the life; no one comes to the Father, but by me.'

'Come to me, all who labour and are heavy laden, and I will give you rest. Take my yoke upon you, and learn from me. . . .'[2]

The great question to which the first part of his teaching led was, 'Who do you say that I am?' He affirmed that Abraham had rejoiced to see his day, that Moses had written of him, that the Scriptures bore witness to him, and that indeed in the

[2] John 6:35; 8:12; 11:25, 26; 14:6; Matthew 11:28, 29.

23

three great divisions of the Old Testament – the law, the prophets and the writings – there were 'things concerning himself'.[3]

Luke describes in some detail the dramatic visit which Jesus paid to the synagogue of his home village, Nazareth. He was given a scroll of the Old Testament Scriptures and he stood up to read. The passage was Isaiah 61:1-2:

> 'The Spirit of the Lord is upon me,
> because he has anointed me to preach
>   good news to the poor.
> He has sent me to proclaim release to the
>   captives
> and recovering of sight to the blind,
> to set at liberty those who are oppressed,
> to proclaim the acceptable year of the Lord.'

He closed the book, returned it to the synagogue attendant and sat down, while the eyes of all the congregation were fastened on him. He then broke the silence with the amazing words, 'Today this scripture has been fulfilled in your hearing.' In other words, 'Isaiah was writing about me.'

With such an opinion of himself, it is not surprising that he called people to himself. Indeed, he did more than issue an invitation; he uttered a command. 'Come to me', he said, and 'Follow me'. If men would only come to him, he promised to lift the burdens of the weary, to satisfy the hungry, and to quench the thirst of the parched soul.[4] Further, his followers were to obey him and to confess him before men. His disciples came to recognize the right of Jesus to make these totalitarian claims, and in their letters Paul, Peter, James and Jude delight to call themselves his 'slaves'.

More than that, he offered himself to his contemporaries as the proper object of their faith and love. It is for man to believe in God; yet Jesus appealed to men to believe in himself. 'This is the work of God,' he declared, 'that you believe in him whom he has sent.' 'He who believes in the Son has

---

[3] Mark 8:29; John 8:56; 5:46; 5:39; Luke 24:27, 44.
[4] Matthew 11:28-30; John 6:35; 7:37.

24

eternal life.' If to believe in him was man's first duty, not to believe in him was his chief sin.[5]

Again, the first and great commandment is to love God with all the heart and soul and mind. Yet Jesus audaciously claimed a man's supreme love. Anyone who loved father, mother, son or daughter more than him was not worthy of him, he said. Indeed, resorting to the vivid Hebrew use of contrast to convey comparison, he added: 'If any one comes to me and does not hate his own father and mother and wife and children and brothers and sisters, yes, and even his own life, he cannot be my disciple.'[6]

So convinced was he of his central place in the purpose of God that he undertook to send One who would take his place after he had returned to heaven. This was the Holy Spirit. Christ's favourite name for him was the Comforter, the 'Paraclete'. It is a legal term, denoting a barrister, an advocate, a counsel for the defence. It would be the Holy Spirit's task to plead the cause of Jesus before the world. 'He will bear witness to me', said Jesus. Again, 'He will glorify me, for he will take what is mine and declare it to you.'[7] So the Holy Spirit's witness to the world and revelation to the church would both concern Jesus Christ.

In one more flash of breath-taking egocentricity, Jesus predicted: 'I, when I am lifted up from the earth, will draw all men to myself.' He knew that the cross would exert a moral magnetism on men and women. But in drawing them, they would be brought primarily neither to God nor to the church, neither to truth nor to righteousness, but to himself. They would in fact be brought to these only by being brought to him.

The most remarkable feature of all this self-centred teaching is that it was uttered by one who insisted on humility in others. He rebuked his disciples for their self-seeking and was wearied by their desire to be great. Did he not practise what he preached?

[5] John 6:29; 3:36; 8:24; 16:8, 9.
[6] Matthew 10:37; Luke 14:26.
[7] John 15:26; 16:14.

He took a little child and set him in the midst as their model. Had he a different standard for himself?

His direct claims

Jesus clearly believed himself to be the Messiah the Old Testament predicted. He had come to establish the kingdom of God foretold by generations of prophets.

It is significant that the first recorded word of his public ministry was the word 'fulfilled', and his first sentence, 'The time has been fulfilled; the kingdom of God has drawn near'. He assumed the title 'Son of man' which was an accepted Messianic title derived originally from one of Daniel's visions. He accepted the description 'Son of God' when challenged by the high priest, which was another Messianic title taken particularly from Psalm 2:7. He also interpreted his mission in the light of the portrayal of the suffering servant of Jehovah in the latter part of the book of Isaiah. The first stage in his instruction of the Twelve culminated in the incident at Caesarea Philippi when Simon Peter confessed his faith in Jesus as the Christ. Others might suppose him to be one of the prophets; but Simon had come to recognize him as the One to whom the prophets pointed. He was not just another signpost, but the destination to which the signposts had led.[8]

The whole ministry of Jesus is coloured by this sense of fulfilment. 'Blessed are the eyes which see what you see!' he once said privately to his disciples. 'For I tell you that many prophets and kings desired to see what you see, and did not see it, and to hear what you hear, and did not hear it.'[9]

But the direct claims with which we are now concerned refer not just to his Messiahship but to his deity. His claim to be the Son of God was more than Messianic; it described the unique and eternal relationship with God which he possessed. Three examples of this greater claim may be given.

First, there is the close association with God as his 'Father'

[8] Mark 1:15, literally; 14:61, 62; 8:27-29.
[9] Luke 10:23, 24; cf. Matthew 13:16, 17.

of which he constantly spoke. Even as a boy of twelve he astonished his human parents by his uncompromising zeal for his heavenly Father's business. And then he made such statements as the following:

'My Father is working still, and I am working.'

'I and the Father are one.'

'I am in the Father and the Father in me.'[10]

It is true that he taught his disciples to address God as 'Father' too, but so different is Christ's sonship from ours that he was obliged to distinguish between them. To him God is 'my Father'. He therefore said to Mary Magdalene, 'I am ascending to my Father and your Father'. It would not have been possible for him to say, 'I ascend to *our* Father.'

These verses are all taken from John's Gospel, but the same unique relationship with God is claimed by Jesus in Matthew 11:27 where he says,

'All things have been delivered to me by my Father; and no one knows the Son except the Father, and no one knows the Father except the Son and any one to whom the Son chooses to reveal him.'

That Jesus did in fact claim this intimate relation to God is further confirmed by the indignation which he aroused in the Jews. He 'made himself the Son of God', they said.[11] So close was his identification with God that it was natural for him to equate a man's attitude to himself with his attitude to God. Thus,

to know him was to know God;
to see him was to see God;
to believe in him was to believe in God;
to receive him was to receive God;
to hate him was to hate God;
to honour him was to honour God.[12]

[10] John 5:17; 10:30; 14:10, 11.
[11] John 19:7.
[12] John 8:19; 14:7; 12:45; 14:9; 12:44; 14:1; Mark 9:37; John 15:23; 5:23.

These are some of the general claims which Jesus made to a unique relationship to God. He also made two more direct claims. The first is recorded at the end of the eighth chapter of John's Gospel. In controversy with the Jews, he said: 'Truly, truly, I say to you, if any one keeps my word, he will never see death.' This was too much for his critics. 'Abraham died,' they expostulated, 'as did the prophets; ... Are you greater than our father Abraham. . . ? Who do you claim to be?'

'Your father Abraham rejoiced that he was to see my day,' Jesus replied.

The Jews were yet more perplexed. 'You are not yet fifty years old, and have you seen Abraham?'

And Jesus responded with one of the most far-reaching claims he ever made: 'Truly, truly, I say to you, before Abraham was, I am.'

Then they took up stones to throw at him.

Now the law of Moses made stoning the penalty of blasphemy, and at first sight one may wonder what they saw to be blasphemous in Christ's words. Of course there was the claim to have lived before Abraham. This he frequently made. He had 'come down' from heaven and 'been sent' by the Father. But that claim was tolerably innocent. We must look further. We notice that he had not said 'Before Abraham was I was', but 'I am'. It was therefore a claim to have been existing eternally before Abraham. But even that is not all. There is more in this 'I am' than a claim to eternity; there is a claim to deity. 'I am' is the divine Name by which Jehovah had revealed himself to Moses, at the burning bush. 'I am who I am ... say this to the people of Israel, "I am has sent me to you".' This divine title Jesus quietly took to himself. It was because of this that the Jews reached out for stones to avenge the blasphemy.

The second example of a direct claim to deity took place after the resurrection (if for the moment we may assume that the resurrection took place). John reports (20:26-29) that on the Sunday following Easter Day, incredulous Thomas was with the other disciples in the upper room when Jesus appeared. He invited Thomas to feel his wounds, and Thomas, overwhelmed with wonder, cried out, 'My Lord and my God!' Jesus accepted the designation. He rebuked Thomas for his unbelief, not for his worship.

His indirect claims

Christ's claim to deity was advanced as forcefully by indirect as by direct means. The implications of his ministry were as eloquent a testimony to his person as his plain statements. On many occasions he exercised functions which belong properly to God. Of these four may be mentioned.

The first is the claim to *forgive sins*. On two separate occasions[13] Jesus forgave sinners. The first time a paralytic was brought to him by his friends and let down on his pallet bed through the roof. Jesus saw that his need was basically spiritual and surprised the crowd by saying to him, 'My son, your sins are forgiven'.

The second declaration of forgiveness was made to a woman known to be immoral. Jesus was taking a meal in a Pharisee's house when she came behind him as he reclined at table, washed his feet with her tears and wiped them with her hair, kissed them and anointed them with ointment. And Jesus said to her, 'Your sins are forgiven'.

On both occasions the bystanders raised their eyebrows and asked, 'Who is this? What blasphemy is this? Who can forgive sins but God only?' Their questions were correctly worded. We may forgive the injuries which others do to us; but the sins we commit against God only God himself can forgive.

Christ's second indirect claim was to *bestow life*. He described himself as 'the bread of life', 'the life' and 'the resurrection and the life'. He likened his followers' dependence on him to the sustenance derived from the vine by its branches. He offered a Samaritan woman 'living water' and promised eternal life to the rich young ruler if he would come and

[13] Mark 2:1-12; Luke 7:36-50.

follow him. He called himself the Good Shepherd who would not only give his life for the sheep but give life to them. He stated that God had given him authority over all flesh, that he should give life to as many as God gave him, and declared, 'the Son gives life to whom he will'.[14]

So definite was this claim that his disciples clearly recognized its truth. It made leaving him impossible. 'To whom shall we go?' asked Peter. 'You have the words of eternal life.'

Life is an enigma. Whether it be physical life or spiritual, its nature is as baffling as its origin. We can neither define what it is nor state where it comes from. We can only call it a divine gift. It is this gift which Jesus claimed to bestow.

Christ's third indirect claim was to *teach the truth*. It is not so much the truths which he taught as the direct and dogmatic manner in which he taught them which calls for notice. His contemporaries were deeply impressed by his wisdom.

> 'Where did this man get all this? What is the wisdom given to him? . . . Is not this the carpenter. . .?'

> 'How is it that this man has learning, when he has never studied?'

But they were even more impressed by his authority.

> 'No man ever spoke like this man.'

> 'His word was with authority.'

> 'When Jesus finished these sayings, the crowds were astonished at his teaching, for he taught them as one who had authority, and not as their scribes.'[15]

If his authority was not that of the scribes, it was not that of the prophets either. The scribes never taught without quoting their authorities. The prophets spoke with the authority of Jehovah. But Jesus claimed an authority of his own. His formula was not 'Thus says the Lord', but 'Truly, truly, I say to you'. It is true that he described his doctrine as

[14] John 6:35; 14:6; 11:25; 15:4,5; 4:10-15; Mark 10: 17, 21; John 10:28; 17:2; 5:21.
[15] Mark 6:3; John 7:15, 46; Luke 4:32; Matthew 7:28, 29.

being not his but the Father's who had sent him. Nevertheless, he knew himself to be such an immediate means of divine revelation as to be able to speak with great personal assurance. He never hesitated or apologized. He had no need to contradict, withdraw or modify anything he said. He spoke the unequivocal words of God: 'he whom God has sent utters the words of God.' He predicted the future with complete conviction. He issued absolute moral commands like 'Love your enemies', 'Do not be anxious about tomorrow', 'Judge not, that you be not judged'. He made promises of whose fulfilment he had no doubt: 'Ask, and it will be given you.' He asserted that his words were as eternal as the law, and would never pass away. He warned his hearers that their destiny depended on their response to his teaching, as the destiny of Israel had depended on their response to Jehovah's word.

Christ's fourth indirect claim was to *judge the world*. This is perhaps the most fantastic of all his statements. Several of his parables imply that he will come back at the end of the world, and that the final day of reckoning will be postponed until his return. He will himself arouse the dead, and all the nations will be gathered before him. He will sit on the throne of his glory, and the judgment will be committed to him by the Father. He will then separate men from one another as a shepherd separates his sheep from his goats. Some will be invited to come and inherit the kingdom prepared for them from the foundation of the world. Others will hear the dreadful words, 'Depart from me, you cursed, into the eternal fire prepared for the devil and his angels'.[16]

Not only will Jesus be the Judge, but the criterion of judgment will be men's attitude to him as shown in their treatment of his 'brethren' or their response to his word. Those who have acknowledged him before men he will acknowledge before his Father: those who have denied him, he will deny. Indeed, for a man to be excluded from heaven on the last day, it will be enough for Jesus to say, 'I never knew you'.[17]

[16] John 5:22, 28, 29; Matthew 25:31-46.
[17] John 12:47, 48; Matthew 10:32, 33; 7:23.

It is hard to exaggerate the magnitude of this claim. Imagine a minister addressing his congregation in these terms today: 'Listen attentively to my words. Your eternal destiny depends on it. I shall return at the end of the world to judge you, and your fate will be settled according to your obedience to me.' Such a preacher would not long escape the attentions of the police or the psychiatrists.

His dramatized claims

It remains for us to consider the recorded miracles of Jesus, which may be described as his dramatized claims.

This is no place for a thorough discussion of the possibility and purpose of miracles. It is sufficient to indicate that the value of Christ's miracles lies less in their supernatural character than in their spiritual significance. They were 'signs' as well as 'wonders'. They were never performed selfishly or senselessly. Their purpose was not to show off or to compel submission. They were not so much demonstrations of physical power as illustrations of moral authority. They are in fact the acted parables of Jesus. They exhibit his claims visually. His works dramatize his words.

John saw this clearly. He constructs his Gospel round six or seven selected 'signs' (see 20:30, 31), and associates them with the great 'I am' declarations which Jesus made. The first sign was the changing of water into wine at a wedding reception in Cana of Galilee. It is not in itself a particularly edifying miracle. Its significance lies beneath the surface. John tells us that the waterpots of stone stood ready 'for the Jewish rites for purification'. This is the clue we are seeking. The water stood for the old religion, like Jacob's well in chapter 4, rich in Old Testament associations. The wine stood for the religion of Jesus. As he changed the water into wine, so the gospel would supersede the law. The sign advanced the claim that he was competent to inaugurate the new order. He was the Messiah. As he was soon to say to the Samaritan woman, 'I . . . am he'.

Similarly, his feeding of the five thousand illustrated his claim to satisfy the hunger of the human heart. 'I am the bread of life,' he said. A little later, he opened the eyes of a man born blind, having previously said, 'I am the light of the world'. If he could restore sight to the blind, he could open men's eyes to see and to know God. Finally, he brought back to life a man called Lazarus who had been dead four days, and claimed, 'I am the resurrection and the life'. He had resuscitated a dead man. It was a sign. The life of the body symbolized the life of the soul. Christ could be the life of the believer before death and would be the resurrection of the believer after death. All these miracles are parables, for men are spiritually hungry, blind and dead, and only Christ can satisfy their hunger, restore their sight and raise them to a new life.[18]

Conclusion

It is not possible to eliminate these claims from the teaching of the carpenter of Nazareth. It cannot be said that they were invented by the evangelists, nor even that they were unconsciously exaggerated. They are widely and evenly distributed in the different Gospels and sources of the Gospels, and the portrait is too consistent and too balanced to have been imagined.

The claims are there. They do not in themselves constitute evidence of deity. The claims may have been false. But some explanation of them must be found. We cannot any longer regard Jesus as simply a great teacher if he was completely mistaken in one of the chief subjects of his teaching – himself. There is a certain disturbing 'megalomania' about Jesus which many scholars have recognized.

'These claims in a mere man would be egoism carried even to imperial megalomania.'[19]

'The discrepancy between the depth and sanity, and (let me add) *shrewdness*, of his moral teaching and the rampant megalomania

[18] John 6:35; 8:12; 11:25.
[19] P. T. Forsyth, *This Life and the Next*, Independent Press, 1947.

which must lie behind his theological teaching unless he is indeed God, has never been satisfactorily got over.'[20]

Was he then a deliberate impostor? Did he attempt to gain the adherence of men to his views by assuming a divine authority he did not possess? This is very difficult to believe. There is something guileless about Jesus. He hated hypocrisy in others and was transparently sincere himself.

Was he sincerely mistaken then? Had he a fixed delusion about himself? This possibility has its protagonists, but one suspects that their delusion is greater than his. Jesus does not give the impression of that abnormality which one expects to find in the deluded. His character appears to support his claims, and it is in this sphere that we must now pursue our investigation.

[20] C. S. Lewis, *Miracles*, Bles, 1947.

3 THE CHARACTER OF CHRIST

Some years ago I received a letter from a young man I knew slightly. 'I have just made a great discovery', he wrote. 'Almighty God had two sons. Jesus Christ was the first; I am the second.' I glanced at the address at the top of his letter. He was writing from a well-known mental hospital.

There have of course been many pretenders to greatness and to divinity. Lunatic asylums are full of deluded people who claim to be Julius Caesar, the Prime Minister, the Emperor of Japan or Jesus Christ. But no-one believes them. No-one is deceived except themselves. They have no disciples, except perhaps their fellow-patients. They fail to convince other people simply because they do not seem to be what they claim to be. Their character does not support their claims.

Now the Christian's conviction about Christ is greatly strengthened by the fact that he does appear to be who he said he was. There is no discrepancy between his words and his deeds. Certainly a very remarkable character would be necessary to authenticate his extravagant claims, but we believe that he displayed just such a character. His character does not prove his claims to be true, but it strongly confirms them. His claims were exclusive. His character was unique. John Stuart Mill called him

'A unique figure, not more unlike all his predecessors than all his followers'.[1]

[1] Quoted by W. H. Griffith Thomas, *Christianity is Christ*, 1909; Church Book Room Press edition, 1948, p. 15.

Carnegie Simpson wrote,

> 'Instinctively we do not class him with others. When one reads
> his name in a list beginning with Confucius and ending with Goethe
> we feel it is an offence less against orthodoxy than against decency.
> Jesus is not one of the group of the world's great. Talk about
> Alexander the Great and Charles the Great and Napoleon the Great
> if you will. . . . Jesus is apart. He is not the Great; he is the Only.
> He is simply Jesus. Nothing could add to that. . . . He is beyond
> our analyses. He confounds our canons of human nature. He compels
> our criticism to overleap itself. He awes our spirits. There is a saying
> of Charles Lamb . . . that "if Shakespeare was to come into this room
> we should all rise up to meet him, but if that Person was to come into
> it, we should all fall down and try to kiss the hem of his garment".'[2]

We are concerned then to show that Jesus stands in a moral
category by himself. To concede that he was 'the greatest man
who ever lived' does not begin to satisfy us. We cannot talk of
Jesus in comparative, or even superlative terms. To us it is a
question not of comparison, but of contrast. 'Why do you call
me good?' he asked the rich young ruler. 'No one is good but
God alone.' 'Exactly', we should have replied. 'It is not that
you are better than other men, nor even that you are the best of
men, but that you are good – good with the absolute goodness
of God.'

The importance of this claim should be clear. Sin is a con-
genital disease among men. We are born with its infection in
our nature. It is a universal complaint. Therefore if Jesus of
Nazareth was without sin, he was not just man as we know
men. If he was sinless, he was distinct from us. He was supernatural.

> 'His character was more wonderful than the greatest miracle.'[3]

> 'This separateness from sinners is not a little, but a stupendous thing;
> it is the presupposition of redemption; it is that very virtue in Christ
> without which He would not be qualified to be a Saviour, but would,
> like us, need to be saved.'[4]

[2] P. Carnegie Simpson, *The Fact of Christ*, 1930; James Clarke edition.
1952, pp. 19-22.   [3] Tennyson, quoted by Carnegie Simpson, p. 62,
[4] James Denney, *Studies in Theology*, Hodder and Stoughton, 9th edition,
1906, p. 41.

It may be helpful to summarize the evidence for the sinlessness of Christ under four headings.

What Christ himself thought

On one or two occasions Jesus stated directly that he was without sin. When a woman was discovered in the act of adultery and was dragged before him, he issued an embarrassing challenge to her accusers, 'Let him who is without sin among you be the first to throw a stone at her.' Gradually they slunk away until there was no-one left. A little later in the same chapter (John 8), it is recorded that Jesus issued another challenge, this time concerning himself: 'Which of you convicts me of sin?' No-one answered. They slipped away when he accused them. But when he invited them to accuse him, he could stay and bear their scrutiny. They were all sinners; he was without sin. He lived a life of perfect obedience to his Father's will. 'I always do', he said, 'what is pleasing to him'. There was nothing boastful about those words. He spoke naturally, with neither fuss nor pretension.

Similarly, by the very nature of his teaching, he placed himself in a moral category by himself. So indeed did the Pharisee in the Temple in his arrogant thanksgiving, 'God, I thank thee that I am not like the rest of men'. But Jesus assumed his uniqueness unself-consciously. He did not need to draw attention to it. It was a fact so obvious to him that it hardly required emphasis. It was implied rather than asserted. All other men were lost sheep; he had come as the Good Shepherd to seek and to save them. All other men were sick with the disease of sin; he was the doctor who had come to heal them. All other men were plunged in the darkness of sin and ignorance; he was the light of the world. All other men were sinners; he was born to be their Saviour and would shed his blood in death for the forgiveness of their sins. All other men were hungry; he was the bread of life. All other men were dead in trespasses and sins; he could be their life now and their resurrection hereafter. All these metaphors express the moral uniqueness of which he was conscious.

It is not surprising, therefore, that although we are told of the temptations of Jesus, we hear nothing of his sins. He never confesses his sins or asks for forgiveness, although he tells his disciples to do so. He shows no consciousness of moral failure. He appears to have no feeling of guilt and no sense of estrangement from God. His baptism was indeed John's 'baptism of repentance'. But John demurred before baptizing Jesus, and Jesus submitted to it not because he was acknowledging himself to be a sinner but 'to fulfil all righteousness', and to begin to identify himself with the sins of others. He himself seems to have lived in unbroken communion with his Father.

This absence of all moral discontent and this sense of unclouded fellowship with God are particularly remarkable for two reasons. The first is that Jesus possessed a keen moral judgment. 'He ... knew what was in man.' Often it is recorded of him in the Gospel narratives that he read the inner questionings and perplexities of the crowd. His clear perception led him fearlessly to expose the duplicity of the Pharisees. He hated their hypocrisy. He pronounced woes upon them as thunderous as those of the Old Testament prophets. Ostentation and pretence were an abomination to him. Yet his penetrating eye saw no sin in himself.

The second reason why his self-conscious purity is astonishing is that it is utterly unlike the experience of all saints and mystics. The Christian knows that the nearer he approaches God, the more he becomes aware of his own sin. In this the saint somewhat resembles the scientist. The more the scientist discovers, the more he appreciates the mysteries which await his discovery. So the more the Christian grows in Christlikeness, the more he perceives the vastness of the distance which still separates him from Christ.

A glance into any Christian biography will satisfy the reader of this fact, if his own experience is not sufficient evidence. One example may be given. David Brainerd was a young pioneer missionary among the Indians of Delaware at the beginning of the nineteenth century. His diary and letters reveal the rich quality of his devotion to Christ. Despite great pain and crippling weakness which led to his death at the age of twenty-nine, he gave himself without reserve to his work. He travelled on horseback through thick forests, preached and taught without rest, slept in the open, and was content with no settled home or family life. His diary is full of expressions of love to 'my dear Indians' and of prayers and praises to his Saviour.

Here surely, one would imagine, is a saint of the first order, whose life and work can have been little tainted by sin. Yet as we turn the pages of his diary, he continually laments his moral 'corruption'. He complains of his lack of prayer and love for Christ. He calls himself 'a poor worm', 'a dead dog', and 'an unspeakably worthless wretch'. This is not because he had a morbid conscience. He simply lived near Christ and was painfully aware of his sinfulness.

> And they who fain would serve thee best
> Are conscious most of wrong within.

Yet Jesus Christ, who lived more closely to God than anybody else has done, was free from all sense of sin.

What Christ's friends said

It is clear then that Jesus believed himself to be sinless, as he believed himself to be the Messiah and the Son of God. But may he not have been mistaken in the former as in the latter? What did his disciples think? Did they share his opinion of himself?

It may be thought that the disciples of Christ were poor witnesses. It has been argued that they were biased, and that they deliberately painted him in more beautiful colours than he deserved. But in this the apostles have been greatly maligned. Their statements cannot be so lightly dismissed.

There are several reasons why we may confidently rely on their evidence.

First, they lived in close contact with Jesus for about three years. They ate and slept together. They experienced the cramped neighbourliness of the same boat. They even had a common purse (and a common bank account can be a fruitful cause of dissension!). The disciples got on one another's nerves. They quarrelled. But they never found in Jesus the sins they found in themselves. Familiarity normally breeds contempt, but not in this case. Indeed, two of the chief witnesses to the sinlessness of Christ are Peter and John (as we shall see later), and they belonged to that inner group (consisting of Peter, James and John) to whom he gave special privileges and a yet more intimate revelation.

Second, the testimony of the apostles in this matter is trustworthy because they were Jews whose minds had been soaked since infancy in the doctrines of the Old Testament. And one Old Testament doctrine which they had certainly assimilated is the universality of human sin:

'They have all gone astray, they are all alike corrupt; there is none that does good, no, not one.'

'All we like sheep have gone astray; we have turned every one to his own way.'

In the light of this biblical teaching they would not easily have attributed sinlessness to anyone.

Third, the apostolic testimony to the sinlessness of Jesus is the more credible because it is indirect. They do not set out to establish the truth that he was without sin. Their remarks are asides. They are discussing some other subject, and add almost as a parenthesis a reference to his sinlessness.

This is what they say. Peter first describes Jesus as 'a lamb without blemish or spot' and then says that he 'committed no sin; no guile was found on his lips'. John roundly declares that all men are sinners, and that if we say we have no sin or have not sinned, we are both liars ourselves and make God a liar too. But he goes on to say that in Christ, who was manifested to take away our sins, 'there is no sin'.[5]

To this testimony of Peter and John we may add the words of Paul and of the author of the Epistle to the Hebrews. They describe Jesus as one who 'knew no sin', but rather was 'holy, blameless, unstained, separated from sinners.' He was indeed 'in every respect . . . tempted as we are'—but 'without sinning'.[6]

What Christ's enemies conceded

We may feel ourselves to be on safer ground when we come to consider what the enemies of Jesus thought of him. They certainly had no bias—at least not in his favour. We read in the Gospels that 'they watched him' and tried to 'entrap him in his talk'. It is well known that when a debate cannot be won by reasoning, controversialists are prone to descend to personal abuse. If arguments are lacking, mud is a good substitute. Even the annals of the church are smudged by the dirt of personal animosities. So it was with the enemies of Jesus.

Mark assembles four of their criticisms (in 2:1—3:6). Their first accusation was *blasphemy*. Jesus had forgiven a man's sins. This was an invasion of divine territory. It was blasphemous arrogance, they said. But to say so is to beg the question. If he were indeed divine, to forgive sins was his prerogative.

Next, they were (they said) horrified by *his evil associations*. He fraternized with sinners. He ate with publicans. He allowed harlots to approach him. No Pharisee would dream of this behaviour. He would gather his skirts around him and recoil from contact with such scum. He would have thought himself righteous for doing so, too. He would not appreciate the grace and tenderness of Jesus who, though 'separate from sinners', yet earned the honoured title 'friend of sinners'.

Their third accusation was that *his religion was frivolous*. He did not fast like the Pharisees, or even like the disciples of

[5] 1 Peter 1:19; 2:22; 1 John 1:8-10; 3:5.
[6] 2 Corinthians 5:21; Hebrews 7:26; 4:15.

John the Baptist. He was 'a glutton and a drunkard' who came 'eating and drinking'. Such an attack hardly deserves a serious refutation. That Jesus was full of joy is true, but there can be no doubt that he took religion seriously.

Fourth, they were incensed by *his sabbath-breaking*. He healed sick people on the sabbath day. And his disciples even walked through the cornfields on the sabbath, plucking, rubbing and eating corn, which the scribes and Pharisees forbade as tantamount to reaping and threshing. Yet no-one can doubt that Jesus was submissive to the law of God. He obeyed it himself, and in controversy he referred his opponents to it as the arbiter. He also affirmed that God had made the sabbath, and that he had made it for man's benefit. But being himself 'lord of the sabbath', he claimed the right to set aside the false traditions of men and to give to God's law its true interpretation.

All these accusations are either trivial or question-begging. So when Jesus was on trial for his life, his detractors had to hire false witnesses against him. But even then they did not agree with one another. In fact, the only charge they could manufacture against him was not moral but political. And as the stately prisoner came before men for a verdict, again and again he was pronounced righteous. Pilate, after several cowardly attempts to evade the issue, publicly washed his hands and declared himself 'innocent of this man's blood'. Herod could find no fault in him. Judas the traitor, filled with remorse, returned the thirty pieces of silver to the priests with the words 'I have sinned in betraying innocent blood'. The penitent thief on the cross rebuked his confederate for his abuse and added, 'this man has done nothing wrong'. Finally, the centurion, having watched Jesus suffer and die, exclaimed, 'Certainly this man was innocent!'[7]

What we can see for ourselves

In assessing the character of Jesus Christ, we do not need to

[7] Matthew 27:24; Luke 23:15; Matthew 27:3, 4; Luke 23:41, 47.

rely only on the testimony of others; we can make our own estimate. The moral perfection which was quietly claimed by him, confidently asserted by his friends and reluctantly acknowledged by his enemies, is clearly exhibited in the Gospels.

We are given ample opportunity to form our own judgment. The picture of Jesus painted by the evangelists is a comprehensive one. True, it depicts largely his public ministry of barely three years. But we are given a glimpse of his boyhood, and Luke twice repeats that during his hidden years at Nazareth he was developing naturally in body, mind and spirit, and was growing in favour with God and man.

We see him withdrawn into privacy with his disciples, and we watch him in the noisy bustle of the crowd. He is brought before us in the Galilean ministry, hero-worshipped by the mob who wanted to take him by force and make him a king, and we follow him into the cloisters of the Jerusalem Temple where Pharisees and Sadducees united in their subtle inquisition. But whether scaling the dizzy heights of success or plunged into the depths of bitter rejection alone, he is the same Jesus. He is consistent. He has no moods. He does not change.

Again, the portrait is balanced. There is in him no trace of the crank. He believes ardently in what he teaches, but he is not a fanatic. His doctrine is unpopular, but he is not eccentric. There is as much evidence for his humanity as for his divinity. He gets tired. He needs to sleep and eat and drink like other men. He experiences the human emotions of love and anger, joy and sorrow. He is fully human. Yet he is no mere man.

Above all, he was unselfish. Nothing is more striking than this. Although believing himself to be divine, he did not put on airs or stand on his dignity. He was never pompous. There was no touch of self-importance about Jesus. He was humble.

It is this paradox which is so baffling, this combination of the self-centredness of his teaching and the unself-centredness of his behaviour. In thought he put himself first; in deed last. He exhibited both the greatest self-esteem and the greatest self-sacrifice. He knew himself to be the Lord of all, but he became their servant. He said he was going to judge the world, but he washed his apostles' feet.

Never has anyone given up so much. It is claimed (by him as well as by us) that he renounced the joys of heaven for the sorrows of earth, exchanging an eternal immunity to the approach of sin for painful contact with evil in this world. He was born of a lowly Hebrew mother in a dirty stable in the insignificant village of Bethlehem. He became a refugee baby in Egypt. He was brought up in the obscure hamlet of Nazareth, and toiled at a carpenter's bench to support his mother and the other children in their home. In due time he became an itinerant preacher, with few possessions, small comforts and no home. He made friends with simple fishermen and publicans. He touched lepers and allowed harlots to touch him. He gave himself away in a ministry of healing, helping, teaching and preaching.

He was misunderstood and misrepresented, and became the victim of men's prejudices and vested interests. He was despised and rejected by his own people, and deserted by his own friends. He gave his back to be flogged, his face to be spat upon, his head to be crowned with thorns, his hands and feet to be nailed to a common Roman gallows. And as the cruel spikes were driven home, he kept praying for his tormentors, 'Father, forgive them; for they know not what they do.'

Such a man is altogether beyond our reach. He succeeded just where we invariably fail. He had complete self-mastery. He never retaliated. He never grew resentful or irritable. He had such control of himself that, whatever men might think or say or do, he would deny himself and abandon himself to the will of God and the welfare of mankind. 'I seek not my own will', he said, and 'I do not seek my own glory'. As Paul wrote, 'For Christ did not please himself.'

This utter disregard of self in the service of God and man is what the Bible calls love. There is no self-interest in love. The essence of love is self-sacrifice. The worst of men is adorned by an occasional flash of such nobility, but the life of Jesus irradiated it with a never-fading incandescent glow.

Jesus was sinless because he was selfless. Such selflessness is love. And God is love.

4 THE RESURRECTION OF CHRIST

We have considered the extravagant claims which Jesus made and the selfless character which he displayed. We are now to examine the evidence for his historical resurrection from the dead.

Clearly, if it is true, the resurrection has great significance. If Jesus of Nazareth rose from the dead, then he was beyond dispute a unique figure. It is not a question of his spiritual survival, nor of his physical resuscitation, but of his conquest of death and his resurrection to a new plane of existence altogether. We do not know of anyone else who has had this experience. Modern man is therefore as scornful as the Athenian philosophers who heard Paul preach on the Areopagus: 'When they heard of the resurrection of the dead, some mocked.'

The argument is not that his resurrection establishes his deity, but that it is consistent with it. It is only to be expected that a supernatural person should come to and leave the earth in a supernatural way. This is in fact what the New Testament teaches and what, in consequence, the church has always believed. His birth was natural, but his conception was supernatural. His death was natural, but his resurrection was supernatural. His miraculous conception and resurrection do not prove his deity, but they are congruous with it.[1]

[1] We are not concerned here with the virgin birth of Jesus, for it is not used in the New Testament to demonstrate his Messiahship or deity, as is the resurrection. The case for the virgin birth is well argued in *The Virgin Birth of Christ* by James Orr, Hodder and Stoughton, 1907, and *The Virgin Birth* by J. Gresham Machen, Marshall, Morgan and Scott, 1936.

Jesus himself never predicted his death without adding that he would rise, and described his coming resurrection as a 'sign'. Paul, at the beginning of his letter to the Romans, wrote that Jesus was 'designated Son of God in power . . . by his resurrection from the dead', and the earliest sermons of the apostles recorded in the Acts repeatedly assert that by the resurrection God has reversed man's sentence and vindicated his Son.

Of this resurrection Luke, who is known to have been a painstaking and accurate historian, says there are 'many proofs'. We may not feel able to go as far as Thomas Arnold who called the resurrection 'the best attested fact in history', but certainly many impartial students have judged the evidence to be extremely good. For instance, Sir Edward Clarke K.C. wrote to the Rev. E. L. Macassey:

'As a lawyer I have made a prolonged study of the evidences for the events of the first Easter Day. To me the evidence is conclusive, and over and over again in the High Court I have secured the verdict on evidence not nearly so compelling. Inference follows on evidence, and a truthful witness is always artless and disdains effect. The Gospel evidence for the resurrection is of this class, and as a lawyer I accept it unreservedly as the testimony of truthful men to facts they were able to substantiate.'

What is this evidence? An attempt may be made to summarize it by four statements.

The body had gone

The resurrection narratives in the four Gospels begin with the visit of certain women early on Easter Sunday morning to the tomb. On arrival they were dumbfounded to discover that the body of the Lord had disappeared.

Not many days later the apostles began to preach that Jesus had risen. It was the main thrust of their message. But they could hardly have expected men to believe them if a few minutes' walk could have taken them to Joseph's tomb where the body of Jesus still lay! No. The tomb was empty. The body had gone. There can be no doubt about this fact. The

47

question is how to explain it.

First, there is the theory that *the women went to the wrong tomb*. It was still dark, and they were dazed with sorrow. They could easily, it is claimed, have made a mistake.

This sounds plausible on the surface, but it hardly bears examination. To begin with, it cannot have been completely dark. It is true that John says the women came 'while it was still dark'. But in Matthew 28:1 it is 'toward the dawn', while Luke says it was 'at early dawn', and Mark distinctly states that 'the sun had risen'.

Further, these women were no fools. At least two of them had seen for themselves where Joseph and Nicodemus had laid the body. They had even watched the whole process of burial, 'sitting opposite the sepulchre'. The same two (Mary Magdalene and Mary the mother of Jesus) returned at dawn, bringing with them Salome, Joanna and 'the other women', so that if one mistook the path or the tomb, she is likely to have been corrected by the others. And if Mary Magdalene went to the wrong place the first time, she can hardly have repeated her error when she returned in the full light of morning and lingered in the garden till Jesus met her.

Besides, no mere sentiment brought them so early to the tomb. They had come on a practical mission. They had bought spices and were going to complete the anointing of their Lord's body, since the approach of the sabbath had made the work so hasty two days previously. These devoted and businesslike women were not the kind to be easily deceived or to give up the task they had come to do. Again, even if *they* mistook the tomb, would Peter and John, who ran to verify their story, make the same mistake, and others who doubtless came later, including Joseph and Nicodemus themselves?

The second explanation of the empty tomb is *the swoon theory*. Those who maintain this view would have us believe that Jesus did not die on the cross, but only fainted. He then revived in the tomb, left it and subsequently made himself known to the disciples.

This theory simply bristles with problems. It is thoroughly

48

perverse. The evidence entirely contradicts it. Pilate was indeed surprised that Jesus was already dead, but he was sufficiently convinced by the centurion's assurance to give Joseph permission to remove the body from the cross. The centurion was certain because he must have been present when 'one of the soldiers pierced his side with a spear, and at once there came out blood and water'. So Joseph and Nicodemus took down his body, wound it in the grave-clothes and laid it in Joseph's new tomb.

Are we then seriously to believe that Jesus was all the time only in a swoon? That after the rigours and pains of trial, mockery, flogging and crucifixion he could survive thirty-six hours in a stone sepulchre with neither warmth nor food nor medical care? That he could then rally sufficiently to perform the superhuman feat of shifting the boulder which secured the mouth of the tomb, and this without disturbing the Roman guard? That then, weak and sickly and hungry, he could appear to the disciples in such a way as to give them the impression that he had vanquished death? That he could go on to claim that he had died and risen, could send them into all the world and promise to be with them unto the end of time? That he could live somewhere in hiding for forty days, making occasional surprise appearances, and then finally disappear without any explanation? Such credulity is more incredible than Thomas' unbelief.

Third, there is the idea that *thieves stole the body*. There is no shred of evidence for this conjecture. Nor is it explained how thieves could have hoodwinked the Roman guard. Nor can one imagine why thieves should have taken the body and left the graveclothes, nor what possible motive they could have had for their action.

Fourth, it has been argued that the *disciples removed the body*. This, Matthew tells us, is the rumour which the Jews spread from the earliest days. He describes how Pilate, having given permission to Joseph to remove Christ's body, received a deputation of chief priests and Pharisees, who said:

'Sir, we remember how that impostor said, while he was still alive,

"After three days I will rise again." Therefore order the sepulchre to be made secure until the third day, lest his disciples go and steal him away, and tell the people, "He has risen from the dead," and the last fraud will be worse than the first.'

Pilate concurred. 'Make it as secure as you can', he said, and the Jews 'made the sepulchre secure by sealing the stone and setting a guard'. Matthew goes on to describe how the stone, the seal and the guard could not prevent the resurrection, and how the guard went into the city to report to the chief priests what had happened. After consultation they bribed the soldiers and said,

'Tell people, "His disciples came by night and stole him away while we were asleep." And if this comes to the governor's ears, we will satisfy him and keep you out of trouble. So they took the money and did as they were directed; and this story has been spread among the Jews to this day.'

But the story does not hold water. Is it likely that a picked guard, whether Roman or Jewish, would all sleep on duty when detailed to watch? And if they did remain awake, how did the women get past them and roll back the stone?

Even supposing the disciples could have succeeded in removing the Lord's body, there is a psychological consideration which is enough to discredit the whole theory. We learn from the first part of the Acts that in their early preaching the apostles concentrated on the resurrection. 'You killed him, but God raised him, and we are witnesses', they kept saying. Are we then to believe that they were proclaiming what they knew to be a deliberate lie? If they had themselves taken the body of Jesus, to preach his resurrection was to spread a known, planned falsehood. They not only preached it; they suffered for it. They were prepared to go to prison, to the flogging post and to death for a fairy-tale.

This simply does not ring true. It is so unlikely as to be virtually impossible. If anything is clear from the Gospels and the Acts, it is that the apostles were sincere. They may have been deceived, if you like, but they were not deceivers. Hypocrites and martyrs are not made of the same stuff.

The fifth and perhaps the least unreasonable (though still hypothetical) explanation of the disappearance of Christ's body is that *the Roman or Jewish authorities took it into their own custody*. They would certainly have had motive enough for doing so. They had heard that Jesus had talked of resurrection, and were afraid of hanky-panky. So (the argument runs), in order to forestall trickery, they took the precaution of confiscating the corpse.

But when it is examined, this conjectural reconstruction of what happened also falls to pieces. We have already seen that within a few weeks of Jesus' death the Christians were boldly proclaiming his resurrection. The news spread rapidly. The new Nazarene movement threatened to undermine the bulwarks of Judaism and to disturb the peace of Jerusalem. The Jews feared conversions; the Romans riots. The authorities had before them one obvious course of action. They could produce the remains of the body and publish a statement of what they had done.

Instead, they were silent and resorted to violence. They arrested the apostles, threatened them, flogged them, imprisoned them, vilified them, plotted against them, and killed them. But all this was entirely unnecessary if they had in their own possession the dead body of Jesus. The church was founded on the resurrection. Disprove the resurrection, and the church would have collapsed. But they could not; the body was not in their possession. The authorities' silence is as eloquent a proof of the resurrection as the apostles' witness.

These are the theories which men have invented to try to explain the emptiness of the tomb and the disappearance of the body. None of them is satisfactory, and for none of them is there any historical evidence. For want therefore of any adequate alternative explanation, perhaps we may be forgiven if we prefer the simple and sober narrative of the Gospels, describing the events of the first Easter Day. The body of Jesus was not removed by men; it was raised by God.

The graveclothes were undisturbed

It is a remarkable fact that the narratives which say that the body of Jesus had gone also tell us that the graveclothes had not gone. It is John who lays particular emphasis on this fact, for he accompanied Peter on that dramatic early morning race to the tomb. The account he gives of this incident (20:1-10) bears the unmistakable marks of first-hand experience. He outran Peter, but on arrival at the tomb he did no more than look in, until Peter came and entered it. 'Then the other disciple, who reached the tomb first, also went in, and he saw and believed.' The question is: What did he see which made him believe? The story suggests that it was not just the absence of the body, but the presence of the graveclothes and, in particular, their undisturbed condition.

Let us try to reconstruct the story.[2] John tells us (19:38-42) that while Joseph begged Pilate for the body of Jesus, Nicodemus 'came bringing a mixture of myrrh and aloes, about a hundred pounds' weight'. Then together 'they took the body of Jesus, and bound it in linen cloths with the spices, as is the burial custom of the Jews'. That is to say, as they wound the linen 'bandages' round his body, they sprinkled the powdered spices into the folds. A separate cloth will have been used for his head.[3] They thus enswathed his body and head, leaving his face and neck bare, according to oriental custom. They then laid the body on a stone slab which had been hewn out of the side of the cave-tomb.

Now supposing we had been present in the sepulchre when the resurrection of Jesus actually took place. What should we have seen? Should we have seen Jesus begin to move, and then yawn and stretch and get up? No. We do not believe that he returned to this life. He did not recover from a swoon. He had died, and he rose again. His was a resurrection, not a resuscitation. We believe that he passed miraculously from

[2] Following Henry Latham, *The Risen Master*, LeightonBell, 1904.

[3] This is clear from John's account of the burial clothes of Lazarus. For when Jesus resuscitated him, 'The dead man came out, his hands and feet bound with bandages, and his face wrapped with a cloth' (11:44).

death into an altogether new sphere of existence. What then should we have seen, had we been there? We should suddenly have noticed that the body had disappeared. It would have 'vaporized', being transmuted into something new and different and wonderful. It would have passed through the graveclothes, as it was later to pass through closed doors, leaving them untouched and almost undisturbed. Almost but not quite. For the body cloths, under the weight of 100lbs. of spices, once the support of the body had been removed, would have subsided or collapsed, and would now be lying flat. A gap would have appeared between the body cloths and the head napkin, where his face and neck had been. And the napkin itself, because of the complicated criss-cross pattern of the bandages, might well have retained its concave shape, a crumpled turban, but with no head inside it.

A careful study of the text of John's narrative suggests that it is just these three characteristics of the discarded graveclothes which he saw. First, he saw the cloths 'lying'. The word is repeated twice, and the first time it is placed in an emphatic position in the Greek sentence. We might translate, 'He saw, as they were lying (or 'collapsed'), the linen cloths.' Next, the head napkin was 'not . . . with the linen cloths but . . . in a place by itself'. This is unlikely to mean that it had been bundled up and tossed into a corner. It lay still on the stone slab, but was separated from the body cloths by a noticeable space. Third, this same napkin was 'not lying . . . but wrapped together. . .'. This last word has been translated 'twirled'. The Authorized Version 'wrapped together' and the Revised Standard Version 'rolled up' are both unfortunate translations. The word aptly describes the rounded shape which the empty napkin still preserved.

It is not hard to imagine the sight which greeted the eyes of the apostles when they reached the tomb: the stone slab, the collapsed graveclothes, the shell of the head-cloth and the gap between the two. No wonder they 'saw and believed'. A glance at these graveclothes proved the reality, and indicated the nature, of the resurrection. They had been neither touched

53

nor folded nor manipulated by any human being. They were like a discarded chrysalis from which the butterfly has emerged.

That the state of the graveclothes was intended to be visible, corroborative evidence for the resurrection is further suggested by the fact that Mary Magdalene (who had returned to the tomb after bringing the news to Peter and John) 'stooped to look into the tomb; and she saw two angels in white, sitting where the body of Jesus had lain, one at the head and one at the feet'. Presumably this means that they sat on the stone slab with the graveclothes between them. Both Matthew and Mark add that one of them said, 'He is not here; for he has risen, as he said. Come, see the place where he lay'.[4] Whether or not the reader believes in angels, these allusions to the place where Jesus had lain, emphasized by both the position and the words of the angels, at least confirms what the understanding of the evangelists was: the position of the clothes and the absence of the body were concurrent witnesses to his resurrection.

The Lord was seen

Every reader of the Gospels knows that they include some extraordinary stories of how Jesus appeared to his disciples after his resurrection. We are told of ten separate appearances of the risen Lord to what Peter calls 'chosen witnesses'. It is said that he appeared to Mary Magdalene, to the women returning from the sepulchre, to Peter, to two disciples on the road to Emmaus, to the ten gathered in the upper room, to the eleven including Thomas a week later, to 'more than five hundred brethren at one time' probably on the mountainside in Galilee, to James, to some disciples including Peter, Thomas, Nathanael, James and John by the Galilee lakeside, and to many on the Mount of Olives near Bethany at the time of the ascension. Paul adds himself at the end of his catalogue in 1 Corinthians 15 of those who saw the risen Jesus, referring

4 John 20:11, 12; Matthew 28:6; Mark 16:6.

to his experience on the Damascus Road. And since Luke tells us at the beginning of the Acts that Jesus 'presented himself alive after his passion by many proofs, appearing to them (the apostles) during forty days', there may well have been other appearances, of which no record has survived.

We cannot lightly dismiss this body of living testimony to the resurrection. We must find some explanation of these narratives. Only three seem possible. One is that they were inventions; the second that they were hallucinations; the third that they were true.

Were they *inventions*? There is no need to devote much space to the refutation of this suggestion. That the resurrection appearance stories are not deliberate inventions is as plain as could be. For one thing the narratives are sober and unadorned; for another they are graphic, and enlivened by the detailed touches which sound like the work of an eye-witness. The stories of the race to the tomb and of the walk to Emmaus are too vivid and real to have been invented.

Besides, no-one could call them good inventions. If we had wanted to invent the resurrection, we might have done much better ourselves. We should have been careful to avoid the complicated jigsaw puzzle of events which the four Gospels together produce. We should have eliminated, or at least watered down, the doubts and fears of the apostles. We should probably have included a dramatic account of the resurrection itself (as do the fantastic apocryphal Gospels), describing the power and glory of the Son of God as he broke the bonds of death and burst from the tomb in triumph. But no-one saw it happen, and we have no description of it. Again, we should scarcely have chosen Mary Magdalene as the first witness, if only to avoid Renan's sneer that 'la passion d'une hallucinée donne au monde un dieu ressuscité'.

There is an objection to the theory of invention greater than the naïvety of the narratives. It is the obvious fact, to which we have already had occasion to refer, that the apostles, and so the evangelists and the early church, were sublimely convinced that Jesus had risen. The whole New Testament breathes an atmosphere of certainty and conquest. Its writers may have been, if you like, tragically misled; they were definitely not deliberately misleading.

If these accounts were not inventions, were the appearances themselves *hallucinations*? This opinion has been widely held and confidently expressed; and of course hallucinations are not an uncommon phenomenon. A hallucination is the 'apparent perception of an external object when no such object is present', and is associated most frequently with someone who is at least neurotic, if not actually psychotic. Most of us have known people who see things and hear voices, and live sometimes or always in an imaginary world of their own. It is not possible to say that the apostles were unbalanced people of this type. Mary Magdalene may have been, but hardly blustering Peter and doubting Thomas.

Hallucinations have also been known to occur in quite ordinary and normal people, and in such cases two characteristics may usually be discerned. First, they happen as the climax to a period of exaggerated wishful thinking. Second, the circumstances of time, place and mood are favourable. There must be the strong inward desire and the predisposing outward setting.

When we turn to the Gospel narratives of the resurrection, however, both these factors are missing. Far from wishful thinking, it was just the opposite. When the women first found the tomb empty, they fled in 'trembling and astonishment' and were 'afraid'. When Mary Magdalene and the other women reported that Jesus was alive, the apostles 'would not believe it', and their words 'seemed to them an idle tale'. When Jesus himself came and stood in their midst 'they were startled and frightened, and supposed that they saw a spirit', so that Jesus 'upbraided them for their unbelief and hardness of heart'. Thomas was adamant in his refusal to believe unless he could actually see and feel the nail-wounds. When later Christ met the eleven and others by appointment on a mountain in Galilee, 'they worshipped him; but some doubted'. Here was no wishful thinking, no naïve credulity, no blind acceptance. The disciples were not gullible, but rather cautious, sceptical and 'slow of heart to believe'. They were not susceptible to hallucinations. Nor would strange visions have satisfied them. Their faith was grounded upon the hard facts of verifiable experience.

Not only so, but the outwardly favourable circumstances were missing too. If the appearances had all taken place in one or two particularly sacred places, which had been hallowed by memories of Jesus, and their mood had been expectant, our suspicions might well be aroused. If we had only the story of the appearances in the upper room, we should have cause to doubt and question. If the eleven had been gathered in that special place where Jesus had spent with them some of his last earthly hours, and they had kept his place vacant, and were sentimentalizing over the magic days of the past, and had remembered his promises to return, and had begun to wonder if he might return and to hope that he would, until the ardour of their expectation was consummated by his sudden appearance, we might indeed fear that they had been mocked by a cruel delusion.

But this was not the case. Indeed, an investigation of the ten appearances reveals an almost studied variety in the circumstances of person, place and mood in which they occurred. He was seen by individuals alone (Mary Magdalene, Peter and James), by small groups and by more than five hundred people together. He appeared in the garden of the tomb, near Jerusalem, in the upper room, on the road to Emmaus, by the lake of Galilee, on a Galilee mountain and on the Mount of Olives.

If there was variety in person and place, there was variety in mood also. Mary Magdalene was weeping; the women were afraid and astonished; Peter was full of remorse, and Thomas of incredulity. The Emmaus pair were distracted by the events of the week and the disciples in Galilee by their fishing. Yet through their doubts and fears, through their unbelief and preoccupation the risen Lord made himself known to them.

It is impossible to dismiss these revelations of the divine

Lord as the hallucinations of deranged minds. So, if they were neither inventions nor hallucinations, the only alternative left is that they actually happened. The risen Lord was seen.

The disciples were changed

Perhaps the transformation of the disciples of Jesus is the greatest evidence of all for the resurrection, because it is entirely artless. They do not invite us to look at themselves, as they invite us to look at the empty tomb and the collapsed graveclothes and the Lord whom they had seen. We can see the change in them without being asked to look. The men who figure in the pages of the Gospels are new and different men in the Acts. The death of their Master left them despondent, disillusioned, and near to despair. But in the Acts they emerge as men who hazard their lives for the name of the Lord Jesus Christ and who turn the world upside down.

What has made the change? What accounts for their new faith and power, joy and love? Partly, no doubt, Pentecost and the coming of the Holy Spirit; but then the Holy Spirit came only when Jesus had risen and ascended. It is as if the resurrection let loose mighty moral and spiritual forces. Two examples stand out.

The first is Simon Peter. During the telling of the Passion story Peter has suffered a tragic eclipse. He has denied Christ three times. He has cursed and sworn as if he had never known the restraining influence of Jesus in his life. He has gone out into the night to weep bitterly. When Jesus is dead, he joins the others in the upper room, behind barred doors 'for fear of the Jews', and is utterly dejected.

But when we turn over one or two pages in the Bible, we see him standing, perhaps on the steps outside the same upper room of the same house in Jerusalem, preaching so boldly and so powerfully to a vast crowd that three thousand people believe in Christ and are baptized. We turn on to the next chapters of the Acts and we watch him defying the very Sanhedrin who had condemned Jesus to death, rejoicing that he is counted worthy to suffer shame for his name, and later sleeping in his cell on the night before his expected execution.

Simon Peter is a new man. The shifting sands have been blown away; true to his nickname, he is a real rock now. What has made the difference?

Or take James, who later assumed a position of leadership in the Jerusalem church. He is one of 'the brethren of the Lord', who throughout the Gospels are represented as not believing in Jesus: 'Even his brothers did not believe in him.' But when we reach the first chapter of the Acts, the list which Luke gives of the assembled disciples concludes with the words 'and ... his brothers'. James is evidently a believer now. What has made the difference? What convinced him? Perhaps we have the clue we are seeking in 1 Corinthians 15:7 where Paul, cataloguing those who had seen the risen Jesus, adds 'he appeared to James'.

It was the resurrection which transformed Peter's fear into courage, and James' doubt into faith. It was the resurrection which changed the sabbath into Sunday and the Jewish remnant into the Christian church. It was the resurrection which changed Saul the Pharisee into Paul the apostle, the fanatical persecutor into a preacher of the very faith he previously tried to destroy. 'Last of all', Paul wrote, '... he appeared also to me.'

These are the evidences for the resurrection. The body had disappeared. The graveclothes remained undisturbed. The Lord was seen. And the disciples were changed. There is no adequate explanation of these phenomena other than the great Christian affirmation 'the Lord is risen indeed'.

*   *   *

We have been occupied for three chapters in a critical investigation of the most absorbing personality of history, a modest carpenter from Nazareth who became a peasant preacher and died a criminal's death.

His claims were stupendous.

He seems to have been morally perfect.

He rose from the dead.

The cumulative weight of this evidence is all but conclusive.

Part Two: Man's Need

5 THE FACT AND NATURE OF SIN

We have given considerable space to an examination of the evidence for the unique deity of Jesus of Nazareth; and we may be convinced that he is the Lord, the Son of God. Yet the preoccupation of the New Testament is not just with who he was, but with what he came to do. He is presented not simply as the Lord from heaven but also as the Saviour of sinners. Indeed, the two cannot be separated, for the validity of his work depends on the divinity of his person.

But in order to appreciate the work which Jesus accomplished, we must understand who *we* are as well as who *he* was. His work was done for us. It was the work of a person for persons, a mission undertaken for needy persons by the only person competent to meet their need. His competence lies in his deity; our need lies in our sin. We have tested his competence; we must now expose our need.

So we turn from Christ to man, from the sinlessness and glory that are in him to the sin and shame that are in us. Only then, after we have clearly grasped what we are, shall we be in a position to perceive the wonder of what he has done for us and offers to us. Only when we have had our malady accurately diagnosed shall we be willing to take the medicine prescribed.

Sin is an unpopular subject, and Christians are often criticized for harping on it too much. But it is only because Christians are realists that they do so. Sin is not a convenient invention of parsons to keep them in their job; it is a fact of human experience.

The history of the last hundred years or so has convinced

many people that the problem of evil is located in man himself, not merely in his society. In the nineteenth century a liberal optimism flourished. It was then widely believed that human nature was fundamentally good, that evil was largely caused by ignorance and bad housing, and that education and social reform would enable men to live together in happiness and goodwill. But this illusion has been shattered by the hard facts of history. Educational opportunities have spread rapidly in the western world, and many welfare states have been created. Yet the atrocities which accompanied both world wars, the subsequent international conflicts, the continuance of political oppression and racial discrimination, and the general increase of violence and crime have forced thoughtful people to acknowledge the existence in every man of a hard core of selfishness.

Much that we take for granted in a 'civilized' society is based upon the assumption of human sin. Nearly all legislation has grown up because human beings cannot be trusted to settle their own disputes with justice and without self-interest. A promise is not enough; we need a contract. Doors are not enough; we have to lock and bolt them. The payment of fares is not enough; tickets have to be issued, inspected and collected. Law and order are not enough; we need the police to enforce them. All this is due to man's sin. We cannot trust each other. We need protection against one another. It is a terrible indictment of human nature.

The universality of sin

The biblical writers are quite clear that sin is universal. 'There is no man who does not sin,' says Solomon in an aside during his great prayer at the dedication of the Temple. 'Surely there is not a righteous man on earth who does good and never sins' adds the Preacher in the book of Ecclesiastes. Several of the psalms lament the universality of human sin. Psalm 14, which describes the godless 'fool', gives a very pessimistic description of human wickedness:

62

'They are corrupt, they do abominable deeds,
　　there is none that does good.
The Lord looks down from heaven
　　　upon the children of men,
　　to see if there are any that act wisely,
　　that seek after God.
They have all gone astray, they are all
　　　alike corrupt;
　　there is none that does good,
　　no, not one.'

The psalmists' conscience tells them that if God were to rise up in judgment against man, none could escape his condemnation. 'If thou, O Lord, shouldst mark iniquities, Lord, who could stand?' Hence the prayer, 'Enter not into judgment with thy servant; for no man living is righteous before thee.'

The prophets are as insistent as the psalmists on the fact that all men are sinners, and no statements are more definite than the two which are to be found in the second half of the book of Isaiah. 'All we like sheep have gone astray; we have turned every one to his own way', and 'We have all become like one who is unclean, and all our righteous deeds are like a polluted garment'.

Nor is this a fancy of Old Testament writers. Paul opens his Epistle to the Romans with a closely reasoned argument, which extends over the first three chapters, that all men indiscriminately, Jews and Gentiles, are sinners in God's sight. He depicts the degraded morals of the pagan world and then adds that the Jew is no better, since, possessing God's holy law himself and teaching it to others, he is yet guilty of breaking it. The apostle then quotes from the psalms and the prophet Isaiah to illustrate his theme, and concludes, 'there is no distinction; since all have sinned and fall short of the glory of God.' John is, if anything, even more explicit when he declares that 'If we say that we have no sin, we deceive ourselves', and 'If we say we have not sinned, we make him a liar'.[1]

But what is sin? Its universal extent is clear; what is its nature? Several words are used in the Bible to describe it. They

[1] Romans 3:22, 23; 1 John 1:8, 10.

group themselves into two categories, according to whether wrongdoing is regarded negatively or positively. Negatively, it is shortcoming. One word represents it as a lapse, a slip, a blunder. Another pictures it as the failure to hit a mark, as when shooting at a target. Yet another shows it to be an inward badness, a disposition which falls short of what is good.

Positively, sin is transgression. One word makes sin the trespass of a boundary. Another reveals it as lawlessness, and another as an act which violates justice.

Both these groups of words imply the existence of a moral standard. It is either an ideal which we fail to reach, or a law which we break. 'Whoever knows what is right to do and fails to do it, for him it is sin', says James. That is the negative aspect. 'Every one who commits sin is guilty of lawlessness; sin is lawlessness', says John. That is the positive aspect.

The Bible accepts the fact that men have different standards. The Jews have the law of Moses. The Gentiles have the law of conscience. But all men have broken the law they know and fallen short of their own standard. What is our ethical code? It may be the law of Moses or the law of Jesus. It may be the decent thing, or the done thing, or the conventions of society. It may be the Buddhist's noble eightfold path or the Muslim's five pillars of conduct. But whatever it is, we have not succeeded in observing it. We all stand self-condemned.

To some good-living people this comes as a genuine surprise. They have their ideals and think they attain them, more or less. They do not indulge in much introspection. They are not unduly self-critical. They know they have had occasional lapses. They are aware of certain character deficiencies. But they are not particularly alarmed by them, and they consider themselves no worse than other men. All this is understandable enough, until we remember two things. First, our sense of failure depends on how high our standards are. It is quite easy to consider oneself good at high-jumping if the bar is never raised more than waist-high. Second, God concerns himself with the thought behind the deed and with the motive behind the action. Jesus clearly taught this in the sermon on the mount.

With these two principles in mind, it should prove a healthy exercise to take the Ten Commandments in Exodus 20 as our standard and see how very far short of it every man falls.

The Ten Commandments

1. *You shall have no other gods before me.*

This is God's demand for man's exclusive worship. It is not necessary to worship the sun, the moon and the stars to break this law. We break it whenever we give to something or someone other than God himself the first place in our thoughts or our affections. It may be some engrossing sport, absorbing hobby, or selfish ambition. Or it may be someone whom we idolize. We may worship a god of gold and silver in the form of safe investments and a healthy bank balance, or a god of wood and stone in the form of property and possessions. None of these things is necessarily wrong in itself. It only becomes wrong when we give to it the place in our lives which belongs only to God. Sin is fundamentally the exaltation of self at the expense of God. What someone wrote of the Englishman is true of everyman: he is 'a self-made man who worships his creator'.

For us to keep this first commandment would be, as Jesus said, to love the Lord our God with all our heart and with all our soul and with all our mind; to make his will our guide and his glory our goal; to put him first in thought, word and deed; in business and leisure; in friendships and career; in the use of our money, time and talents; at work and at home. No man has ever kept this commandment except Jesus of Nazareth.

2. *You shall not make for yourself a graven image.*

If the first commandment concerns the object of our worship, the second concerns its manner. In the first God demands our exclusive worship, and in the second our sincere and spiritual worship. For 'God is spirit, and those who worship him must worship in spirit and truth'.[2]

We may never have manufactured some gruesome metal

[2] John 4:24.

image with our hands, but what hideous mental image do we hold in our minds? Further, although this commandment does not forbid the use of all external forms in worship, it implies that they are useless unless there is inward reality as well. We may have attended church; have we ever really worshipped God? We may have said prayers; have we ever really prayed? We may have read the Bible; have we ever let God speak to us through it and done what he said? It is no good approaching God with our lips if our hearts are far from him.[3] To do so is sheer humbug.

3. *You shall not take the name of the Lord your God in vain.*

The name of God represents the nature of God. There is much in the Bible which commands us to reverence his name, and in the Lord's Prayer we are taught to pray that his name may be hallowed. His holy name can be profaned by our loose language, and most of us could do worse than revise our vocabulary from time to time. But to take God's name in vain is not just a matter of words, but also of thoughts and deeds. Whenever our behaviour is inconsistent with our belief, or our practice contradicts our preaching, we take God's name in vain. To call God 'Lord' and disobey him is to take his name in vain. To call God 'Father' and be filled with anxiety and doubts is to deny his name. To take God's name in vain is to talk one way and act another. This is hypocrisy.

4. *Remember the sabbath day, to keep it holy.*

The Jews' sabbath and the Christians' Sunday are a divine institution. To set one day in seven apart is not just a human arrangement or a social convenience. It is God's plan. He made the sabbath for man, Jesus emphasized,[4] and since he also made the man for whom he made the sabbath, he adapted it to man's need. Man's body and mind need rest, and man's spirit needs the opportunity for worship. The sabbath is therefore a day of rest and a day of worship.

Not only are we to keep it as such ourselves, for our own

[3] Isaiah 29:13; Mark 7:6.
[4] Mark 2:27.

66

good, but we are to do all we can for the common good to ensure that others do not have to work unnecessarily on this day.

So Sunday is a 'holy' day, set apart for God. It is the Lord's day, not our day. It is therefore to be spent in his way, not in ours, for his worship and service and not just for our selfish pleasure.

5. *Honour your father and your mother.*

This fifth commandment still belongs to the first half of the law which concerns our duty to God. For our parents, at least while we are children, stand towards us *in loco Dei*: they represent God's authority. Yet often it is in their own homes that people, young people especially, are at their most selfish and inconsiderate. It is all too easy to be ungrateful and neglectful, and to fail to show our parents due respect and affection. How often do we write to them or visit them? Or do they need financial support which we could give but deny them?

6. *You shall not kill.*

This is not just a prohibition of murder. If looks could kill, many would kill with a look. If murder can be committed by cutting words, many are guilty. Indeed Jesus said that to be angry with someone without a cause, and to be insulting, are just as serious, while John draws the right conclusion when he writes, 'Any one who hates his brother is a murderer'. Every loss of temper, every outburst of uncontrolled passion, every stirring of sullen rage, every bitter resentment and thirsting for revenge - all these things are murder. We can kill by malicious gossip. We can kill by studied neglect and cruelty. We can kill by spite and jealousy. We have probably all done so.

7. *You shall not commit adultery.*

Again, this commandment has a far wider application than just to unfaithfulness in marriage. It includes any sort of sex outside the marriage relationship for which it was designed. It includes flirting, experimenting, and solitary sexual experience. It also includes all sexual perversions, for although men and women are not responsible for a perverted instinct, they are for its indulgence. It includes selfish demands within wedlock, and many, if not all, divorces. It includes the deliberate reading of pornographic literature, and giving in to impure fantasies. Jesus made this clear when he said, '. . . every one who looks at a woman lustfully has already committed adultery with her in his heart'.

Just as to entertain murderous thoughts in the heart is to commit murder, so to entertain adulterous thoughts in the heart is to commit adultery. This commandment in fact embraces every abuse of a sacred and beautiful gift of God.

8. *You shall not steal.*

To steal is to rob a person of anything which belongs to him or is due to him. The theft of money or property is not the only infringement of this commandment. Tax evasion is robbery. So is dodging the customs. So is working short hours. What the world calls 'scrounging' God calls stealing. To overwork and underpay one's staff is to break this commandment. There must be few of us, if any, who have been consistently and scrupulously honest in personal and business affairs. As Arthur Hugh Clough wrote:

> 'Thou shalt not kill', but need'st not strive
> Officiously to keep alive;
> 'Thou shalt not steal' – an empty feat
> When it's more lucrative to cheat.

These negative commandments also imply a positive counterpart. In order truly to abstain from killing, one must do all in one's power to foster the health and preserve the life of others. To refrain from the act of adultery is insufficient. The commandment requires the right, healthy and honourable attitude of each sex towards the other. Similarly, to avoid stealing is no particular virtue if one is miserly or mean. Paul was not satisfied that a thief should stop stealing; he had to start working. Indeed, he had to continue in honest labour until he found himself in a position to give to those in need.

9. *You shall not bear false witness against your neighbour.*
The last five commandments express that respect for the rights of others which is implicit in true love. To break these commandments is to rob a man of the things most precious to him, his life ('you shall not kill'), his home or honour ('you shall not commit adultery'), his property ('you shall not steal'), and now his reputation ('you shall not bear false witness against your neighbour').

This commandment is not only applicable to the lawcourts. It does include perjury. But it also includes all forms of scandal, slander, idle talk and tittle-tattle, all lies and deliberate exaggerations or distortions of the truth. We can bear false witness by listening to unkind rumours as well as by passing them on, by making jokes at somebody else's expense, by creating false impressions, by not correcting untrue statements, and by our silence as well as by our speech.

10. *You shall not covet.*
The tenth commandment is in some ways the most revealing of all. It turns the decalogue from an outward legal code into an inward moral standard. The civil law cannot touch us for covetousness but only for theft. For covetousness belongs to the inner life. It lurks in the heart and the mind. What lust is to adultery and temper is to murder, that covetousness is to theft.

The particular things which we are not to covet and which are mentioned in the commandment are surprisingly modern. In the housing shortage there is much coveting of our neighbour's house, and the divorce courts would not be so full if men did not covet their neighbour's wife. 'Covetousness . . . is idolatry' wrote Paul, and by contrast, 'There is great gain in godliness with contentment'.

Listing these commandments has brought to light an ugly catalogue of sins. So much takes place beneath the surface of our lives, in the secret places of our minds, which other people do not see and which we manage even to conceal from ourselves. But God sees these things. His eye penetrates into the deep recesses of our hearts: 'Before him no creature is hidden, but all are open and laid bare to the eyes of him with whom we have to do.' He sees us as we really are, and his law shows up our sins for what they really are. Indeed, it was the purpose of the law to expose sin, for 'through the law comes knowledge of sin'.

When C. H. Spurgeon, the famous nineteenth-century preacher, was only fourteen, he experienced a tremendous sense of his own sinfulness. Two truths came home to him as never before: 'God's majesty and my sinfulness.' He had a crushing sense of his unworthiness.

> 'I do not hesitate to say that those who examined my life would not have seen any extraordinary sin, yet as I looked upon *myself* I saw outrageous sin against God. I was not like other boys, untruthful, dishonest, swearing and so on. But of a sudden, I met Moses carrying the law . . . God's Ten Words . . . and as I read them, they all seemed to join in condemning me in the sight of the thrice holy Jehovah.'

In our case, too, nothing can convince us of our sinfulness like the lofty, righteous law of God.

6 THE CONSEQUENCES OF SIN

We have seen something of the nature and the universality of human sin. We should like to leave this distasteful subject and pass on immediately to the good news of Christ's salvation, but we are not yet ready to do so. We need to grasp what the results of sin are before we can appreciate what God has done for us and is offering to us in Christ.

Is sin really so very serious? Its evil consequences can best be understood when its effects are seen upon God, upon ourselves and upon our fellow men.

Alienation from God

Even if we do not realize the fact now, the most terrible result of sin is that it cuts us off from God. Man's highest destiny is to know God, to be in personal relationship with him. Our chief claim to nobility as human beings is that we were made in the image of God and are therefore capable of knowing him. But this God whom we are meant to know and whom we ought to know is a righteous Being, infinite in his moral perfection. Scripture lays much stress on this truth:

> 'For thus says the high and lofty One
>   who inhabits eternity, whose name is Holy:
> "I dwell in the high and holy place . . . " '

'The King of kings and Lord of lords, who . . . dwells in unapproachable light.'

'God is light and in him is no darkness at all. If we say we have fellowship with him while we walk in darkness, we lie and do not live according to the truth.'

> 'Our God is a consuming fire.'
>
> 'Who among us can dwell with the devouring fire?
> Who among us can dwell with everlasting burnings?'
>
> 'Thou who art of purer eyes than to behold evil
> and canst not look on wrong.'[1]

All those men of God in the Bible who have caught a glimpse of God's glory have shrunk from the sight in an overwhelming consciousness of their own sins. *Moses*, to whom God appeared in the bush that burned but was not consumed, 'hid his face, for he was afraid to look at God.' *Job*, to whom God spoke 'out of the whirlwind' in words which exalted his transcendent majesty, cried out, 'I had heard of thee by the hearing of the ear, but now my eye sees thee; therefore I despise myself, and repent in dust and ashes.' *Isaiah*, a young man at the threshold of his career, had a vision of God as the King of Israel 'sitting upon a throne, high and lifted up', surrounded by worshipping angels who sang of his holiness and glory, and said, 'Woe is me! For I am lost; for I am a man of unclean lips, and I dwell in the midst of a people of unclean lips; for my eyes have seen the King, the Lord of hosts!' When *Ezekiel* received his strange vision of living winged creatures and whirring wheels, and above them a throne, and on the throne One like a man, enveloped in the brightness of fire and of the rainbow, he recognized it as 'the appearance of the likeness of the glory of the Lord', and he added, 'When I saw it, I fell upon my face.' *Saul of Tarsus,* travelling to Damascus, mad with rage against the Christians, was struck to the ground and blinded by a brilliant light which flashed from heaven more brightly than the noonday sun, and wrote later of his vision of the risen Christ, 'He appeared also to me.' The aged *John*, exiled on the island of Patmos, describes in detail his vision of the risen and glorified Jesus, whose 'eyes were like a flame of fire' and whose 'face was like the sun shining in full strength', and he tells us, 'When I saw him, I fell at his feet as though dead.'[2]

[1] Isaiah 57:15; 1 Timothy 6:15, 16; 1 John 1:5, 6; Hebrews 12:29 (Deuteronomy 4:24); Isaiah 33:14; Habakkuk 1:13.
[2] Exodus 3:1-6; Job 42:5, 6; Isaiah 6:1-5; Ezekiel 1:26-28; Acts 9:1-9; 1 Corinthians 15:8; Revelation 1:9-17.

If the curtain which veils the unspeakable majesty of God could be drawn aside but for a moment, we too should not be able to bear the sight. As it is, we only dimly perceive how pure and brilliant must be the glory of almighty God. However, we know enough to realize that sinful man while still in his sins can never approach this holy God. A great chasm yawns between God in his righteousness and man in his sin. 'What partnership have righteousness and iniquity? Or what fellowship has light with darkness?' asks Paul.

That sin cuts us off from God was brought home dramatically in the Old Testament in the construction of the Tabernacle and the Temple. Both were made in two compartments, the first and larger being called the Holy Place, while the further and smaller was known as the Most Holy Place or the Holy of Holies. In this inner sanctuary was the Shekinah glory, the visible symbol of God's presence. Between the two was the 'veil', a thick curtain which barred access into the Holy of Holies. No-one was allowed to pass through into God's presence except the high priest, and he only on the annual Day of Atonement and then only if he took with him the blood of a sacrifice for sins.

What was thus visibly demonstrated to the Israelites is taught by Old and New Testament writers. Sin brings inevitable separation, and this separation is 'death', spiritual death, the severance of a person from God, the only source of true life. 'The wages of sin is death.'

Further, if in this world we deliberately reject Jesus Christ through whom alone we may find eternal life, we will die eternally in the next world. Hell is a grim and dreadful reality. Let no man deceive you. Jesus himself spoke of it. He called it 'outer darkness' because it is an infinite separation from God who is light. It is also called in the Bible 'the second death' and 'the lake of fire', terms which describe symbolically the forfeiture of eternal life and the ghastly thirst of the soul which are involved in irrevocable banishment from God's presence.[3]

This separation from God which is caused by sin is not only

[3] See, for instance, Matthew 25:30; Revelation 20:14, 15; Luke 16:19-31.

73

taught in the Bible; it is confirmed by human experience. I can still remember my own perplexity when as a boy I said my prayers and tried to penetrate into God's presence. I could not understand why God seemed shrouded in mists and I could not get near him. He seemed remote and aloof. I know the reason now. Isaiah has given me the answer:

> 'Behold, the Lord's hand is not shortened, that
>   it cannot save,
>   or his ear dull, that it cannot hear;
> but your iniquities have made a separation
>   between you and your God,
> and your sins have hid his face from you
>   so that he does not hear.'[4]

We are tempted to say to God, as in the Book of Lamentations, 'Thou hast wrapped thyself with a cloud so that no prayer can pass through.' But in fact God is not responsible for the cloud. We are. Our sins blot out God's face from us as effectively as the clouds do the sun.

Many people have confessed to me that they have had the same desolate experience. Sometimes, in emergencies, in danger, in joy or in the contemplation of beauty, God seems to them to be near, but more often than not they are aware of an inexplicable awayness from God, and they feel abandoned. This is not just a feeling; it is a fact. Until our sins are forgiven, we are exiles, far from our true home. We have no communion with God. In biblical terms we are 'lost', or 'dead through the trespasses and sins' which we have committed.

It is this that accounts for the restlessness of men and women today. There is a hunger in the heart of man which none but God can satisfy, a vacuum which only God can fill. The demand for sensational news in the press and for extravagant love or crime stories at the pictures; pools and pubs; the dirt track and the dog track; the current epidemic of drugs, sex and violence—all these things are symptoms of man's search for satisfaction. They betray his thirst for and separation from God. Augustine was right in the oft-quoted words which

[4] Isaiah 59:1, 2.

74

come near the beginning of his *Confessions*: 'Thou hast made us for thyself, and our hearts are restless till they rest in thee.' This situation is tragic beyond words. Man is missing the destiny for which God made him.

Bondage to self

Sin does not only estrange; it enslaves. If it alienates us from God, it also brings us into captivity.

We need now to consider the 'inwardness' of sin. It is more than an unfortunate outward act or habit; it is a deep-seated inward corruption. In fact, the sins we commit are merely outward and visible manifestations of this inward and invisible malady, the symptoms of a moral disease. The metaphor Jesus used, however, is that of the tree and its fruit. The kind of fruit a tree bears, he said (whether figs or grapes, for example) and their condition (whether good or bad) depend on the nature and health of the tree itself. Just so 'out of the abundance of the heart the mouth speaks'.

In this respect Jesus Christ is at issue with many modern social reformers and revolutionaries. Certainly we are all influenced for good or ill by our education and environment, and by the political and economic system under which we live. Certainly too we should seek justice, freedom and well-being for all men. Yet it was not to a lack of these that Jesus attributed the evils of human society, but to man's very nature, what he called our 'heart'. Here are his exact words:

> 'For from within, out of the heart of man, come evil thoughts, fornication, theft, murder, adultery, coveting, wickedness, deceit, licentiousness, envy, slander, pride, foolishness. All these evil things come from within, and they defile a man.'[5]

The Old Testament had already taught this truth. As Jeremiah put it, 'The heart is deceitful above all things, and desperately corrupt; who can understand it?' Indeed, the Bible is full of references to this infection of human nature or 'original sin'. It is a tendency or bias of self-centredness, which we

[5] Mark 7:21–23.

inherit, which is rooted deeply in our human personality, and which manifests itself in a thousand ugly ways. Paul called it 'the flesh', and gives an inventory of its 'works', or products.

'Now the works of the flesh are plain: immorality, impurity, licentiousness, idolatry, sorcery, enmity, strife, jealousy, anger, selfishness, dissension, party spirit, envy, drunkenness, carousing, and the like.'[6]

Because sin is an inward corruption of human nature we are in bondage. It is not so much certain acts or habits which enslave us, but rather the evil infection from which these spring. So many times in the New Testament we are described as 'slaves'. We resent it but it is true. Jesus aroused the indignation of certain Pharisees when he said to them, 'If you continue in my word, you are truly my disciples, and you will know the truth, and the truth will make you free.'

They retorted, 'We are descendants of Abraham, and have never been in bondage to anyone. How is it that you say, "You will be made free"?'

Jesus answered them, 'Truly, truly, I say to you, every one who commits sin is a slave to sin'.

Paul several times in his Epistles describes the humiliating servitude into which sin brings us.

'You . . . were once slaves of sin.'

'We all once lived in the passions of our flesh, following the desires of body and mind.'

'We ourselves were once foolish, disobedient, led astray, slaves to various passions and pleasures.'[7]

The example of our lack of self-mastery which James gives is the difficulty we have in controlling our tongue. In a well-known chapter full of graphic metaphor he says that if a man 'makes no mistakes in what he says he is a perfect man, able to bridle the whole body also'. He points out that 'the tongue is a little member and boasts of great things'. Its influence spreads like fire; it 'is a restless evil' and is 'full of deadly poison'. We

[6] Galatians 5:19-21.
[7] Romans 6:17; Ephesians 2:3; Titus 3:3.

can tame all kinds of beasts and birds, he adds, 'but no human being can tame the tongue'.[8]

We know this only too well. We have high ideals but weak wills. We want to live a good life, but we are chained in the prison of our self-centredness. However much we may boast of being free, we are in reality but slaves. We need to come in tears to God and say:

> 'It is not finished, Lord,
> There is not one thing done,
> There is no battle of my life
> That I have really won.
> And now I come to tell thee
> How I fought to fail,
> My human, all too human, tale
> Of weakness and futility.'[9]

It is no use giving us rules of conduct; we cannot keep them. Let God go on saying 'Thou shalt not', yet we shall to the end of time. A lecture will not solve our problem; we need a Saviour. The education of the mind is not enough without a change of heart. Man has found the secret of physical power, the power of nuclear reaction. Now he needs spiritual power, to set him free from himself, to conquer and control himself, the power to give him moral character to match his scientific achievement.

Conflict with others

Still our list of the terrible consequences of sin is not complete. There is one more to consider, its effect on our relationships with others.

We have seen that sin is a deep-seated infection of nature. It lies at the root of our personality. It controls our ego. In fact, sin is self. And all the sins we commit are assertions of the self against either God or man. The ten commandments, although a series of negative prohibitions, set forth our duty to God and to others. This is even more clear in the positive summary of

[8] James 3:1-12.
[9] Studdert Kennedy.

the law which Jesus made by joining a verse from Leviticus (19:18) to a verse from Deuteronomy (6:5): 'You shall love the Lord your God with all your heart, and with all your soul, and with all your mind. This is the great and first commandment. And a second is like it, You shall love your neighbour as yourself. On these two commandments depend all the law and the prophets'.

It is important to observe that the first commandment concerns our duty to God, and not our duty to our neighbour. We are to love God first; and then we are to love our neighbour as ourselves. So God's order is that we put him first, others next, self last. Sin is the reversal of the order. It is to put ourselves first, our neighbour next, and God somewhere in the background. The man who wrote his autobiography and entitled it *Dear Me* was only giving expression to what we all think of ourselves. When the ice-cream is brought into the children's party the cry goes up 'Me first!' As we grow up we learn not to say that kind of thing; but we still think it. Archbishop William Temple's definition of original sin perfectly describes this truth:

'I am the centre of the world I see; where the horizon is depends on where I stand. . . . Education may make my self-centredness less disastrous by widening my horizon of interest; so far it is like climbing a tower, which widens the horizon for physical vision, while leaving me still the centre and stand..rd of reference.'[10]

This basic self-centredness affects all our behaviour. We do not find it easy to adjust to other people. We tend either to despise them or to envy them, to have either superiority or inferiority feelings. For we seldom think of ourselves with that 'sober judgment' which Paul urged upon his readers. Sometimes we are full of self-pity, at other times of self-esteem, self-will or self-love.

All the relationships of life are complicated – parents and children, husband and wife, employer and employed. Juvenile delinquency no doubt has many causes, and much is due to lack of security in the home; but the fact is that delinquents are (for

10 *Christianity and Social Order*, 1942; SCM Press edition, 1950, pp. 36-37.

whatever reason) asserting themselves against society. Hundreds of divorces could be prevented if people were humble enough to blame themselves more than their partner. Whenever couples have been to see me because their marriage was threatened, I have noticed that each tells a different story – a story sometimes so different that one would not guess they described the same situation unless one knew.

Most quarrels are due to a misunderstanding, and the misunderstanding is due to our failure to appreciate the other man's point of view. It is more natural to us to talk than to listen, to argue than to submit. This is true in industrial disputes as much as in domestic quarrels. Many management-worker conflicts could be resolved if both sides first examined themselves critically and then examined the other side charitably, instead of which we are always charitable to ourselves and critical of others. The same could be said of complex international unrest. The tensions of today are due largely to fear and folly. Our outlook is onesided. We exaggerate our own virtue and the other man's vice.

It is easy to write this condemnation of social relationships today. The only reason for doing so is to show how human sin or self-centredness is the cause of all our troubles. It brings us into conflict with each other. If only the spirit of self-assertion could be replaced by the spirit of self-sacrifice, our conflicts would cease. And self-sacrifice is what the Bible means by 'love'. While sin is possessive, love is expansive. Sin's characteristic is the desire to get; love's characteristic is the desire to give.

> 'Love ever gives,
> Forgives, outlives,
> And ever stands with open hands,
> And while it lives it gives.
> For this is love's prerogative,
> To give – and give – and give.'

What man needs is a radical change of nature, what Professor H. M. Gwatkin has called 'a change from self to unself'. Man cannot work it within himself. He cannot operate on himself. Again, he needs a Saviour.

Part Three: Christ's Work

7 THE DEATH OF CHRIST

Christianity is a rescue religion. It declares that God has taken the initiative in Jesus Christ to deliver us from our sins. This is the main theme of the Bible.

> 'You shall call his name Jesus, for he will save his people from their sins.'

> 'The Son of man came to seek and to save the lost.'

> 'The saying is sure and worthy of full acceptance, that Christ Jesus came into the world to save sinners.'

> 'We have seen and testify that the Father has sent his Son as the Saviour of the world.'[1]

More particularly, since sin has three principal consequences, as we have seen, 'salvation' includes man's liberation from them all. Through Jesus Christ the Saviour we can be brought out of exile and reconciled to God; we can be born again, receive a new nature and be set free from our moral bondage; and we can have the old discords replaced by a fellowship of love. The first aspect of salvation Christ made possible by his suffering of death, the second by the gift of his Spirit and the third by the building of his church. The first will occupy our thought in this chapter; the second and third in the next.

Paul described his work as a 'ministry of reconciliation' and his gospel as a 'message of reconciliation'. He also made it quite clear where this reconciliation comes from. God is its author, he says, and Christ its agent. 'All this is from God, who through Christ reconciled us to himself.' Again, 'God was in Christ

[1] Matthew 1:21; Luke 19:10; 1 Timothy 1:15; 1 John 4:14.

reconciling the world to himself.' All that was achieved through the death of Jesus on the cross had its origin in the mind and heart of the eternal God. No explanation of Christ's death or man's salvation which fails to do justice to this fact is loyal to the teaching of the Bible. 'God so loved the world that he gave his only Son, that whoever believes in him should not perish but have eternal life.' Again, 'in him all the fulness of God was pleased to dwell, and through him to reconcile to himself all things, whether on earth or in heaven, making peace by the blood of his cross.'[2]

But what does this 'reconciliation' mean? The same word is translated 'atonement' in Romans 5:11 (AV), and an 'atonement' denotes either an action by which two conflicting parts are made 'at one' or the state in which their oneness is enjoyed and expressed. This 'atonement', Paul says, we have 'received' through our Lord and Saviour Jesus Christ. We have not ourselves achieved it by our own effort; we have received it from him as a gift. Sin caused an estrangement; the cross, the crucifixion of Christ, has accomplished an atonement. Sin bred enmity; the cross has brought peace. Sin created a gulf between man and God; the cross has bridged it. Sin broke the fellowship; the cross has restored it. To state the same truth in different words, as Paul did to the Romans, 'the wages of sin is death, but the free gift of God is eternal life in Christ Jesus our Lord'.

But why was the cross necessary for our salvation? Is it really vital to Christianity? What exactly did it achieve? The centrality and meaning of the cross are what we must now go on to consider.

The centrality of the cross

In order to grasp that the death of Jesus as a sacrifice for sin is central to the message of the Bible we must first go back to the Old Testament. Old Testament religion was sacrificial from the beginning. Ever since Abel brought lambs from his flock and

[2] John 3:16; Colossians 1:19, 20.

'the Lord had regard for Abel and his offering', worshippers of Jehovah brought sacrifices to him. Altars were built, animals were killed and blood was shed long before the laws of Moses. But under Moses, after the covenant had been ratified between God and the people at Mount Sinai, what had been somewhat haphazard was regularized by divine ordinance.

The great prophets of the eighth and seventh centuries BC protested against the formalism and immorality of the worshippers, but the sacrificial system continued without interruption until the destruction of the Temple in AD 70. Every Jew was familiar with the ritual attached to burnt offering, trespass offering and their appropriate drink offerings, as well as with the special occasions, daily, weekly, monthly and yearly when they had to be offered. No Jew could have failed to learn the fundamental lessons of all this educative process that 'the life of the flesh is in the blood' and that 'without the shedding of blood there is no forgiveness of sins.'[3]

The Old Testament sacrifices foreshadowed the sacrifice of Christ in visible symbol; the prophets and psalmists foretold it in words. We can see him in the persecuted but innocent victim described in certain psalms which were later applied to Jesus. We detect him in Zechariah's shepherd who is smitten and whose sheep are scattered abroad, and in Daniel's prince or 'anointed one' who is 'cut off'. Above all, we can find him in the noble figure who appears in the Servant Songs towards the end of the prophecy of Isaiah, the suffering servant of Jehovah, the despised 'man of sorrows', who is wounded for the transgressions of others, is led like a lamb to the slaughter and bears the sins of many. Truly, 'thus it is written, that the Christ should suffer'.[4]

When Jesus came, he knew himself to be a son of destiny. He recognized that the Scriptures were bearing witness to him and that it was in him that their expectation was to be fulfilled. This is particularly clear in reference to his coming sufferings. The turning point of his ministry came at Caesarea Philippi

[3] Leviticus 17:11; Hebrews 9:22.

[4] Zechariah 13:7; cf. Mark 14:27; Daniel 9:25, 26; Isaiah 53; Luke 24:46.

when, immediately after Simon Peter had confessed him to be the Christ, 'he began to teach them that the Son of man must suffer many things'.

It is this 'must', this sense of compulsion laid upon him by the Scriptures as revealing the Father's will, which continually recurs in his teaching. He had 'a baptism to be baptized with' and felt himself constrained until it was accomplished. He kept moving steadily towards what he called his 'hour', which in the Gospel narrative is said several times not to have come, and of which at last, shortly before his arrest, with the cross in sight, he could say, 'Father, the hour has come'.

The prospect of the ordeal before him filled him with foreboding. 'Now is my soul troubled', he cried out. 'And what shall I say, "Father, save me from this hour"? No, for this purpose I have come to this hour. Father, glorify thy name.' When at last the moment of his arrest arrived, and Simon lunged out with his sword to protect him, slashing the ear of the high priest's servant, Jesus rebuked him, 'Put your sword into its sheath; shall I not drink the cup which the Father has given me?' According to Matthew, Jesus added, 'Do you think that I cannot appeal to my Father, and he will at once send me more than twelve legions of angels? But how then should the scriptures be fulfilled, that it must be so?'[5]

The supreme importance of the cross which the Old Testament foretold and Jesus taught is fully recognized by the New Testament authors. The writers of the four Gospels devote a disproportionate amount of space to Christ's last week and death in comparison to the rest of his life and ministry. Two-fifths of the first Gospel, three-fifths of the second, one-third of the third, and almost one-half of the fourth, are given to an account of the events between his triumphal entry into Jerusalem and his triumphant ascension into heaven. It is particularly striking in the case of John, whose Gospel has sometimes been divided into two equal halves which have been entitled 'The Book of the Signs' and 'The Book of the Passion'.

[5] Mark 8:31; Luke 12:50; John 17:1; 12:27, 28; 18:11; Matthew 26:53, 54.

What is implied in the Gospels is stated explicitly in the Epistles, and most notably by Paul. The apostle never grew tired of reminding his readers of the cross. He had himself a vivid sense of indebtedness to the Saviour who had died for him. 'The Son of God . . . loved me', he could write, 'and gave himself for me', and therefore, 'far be it from me to glory except in the cross of our Lord Jesus Christ.'

To the Corinthians, who were in danger of being entangled in the subtleties of Greek philosophy, the apostle wrote, 'Jews demand signs and Greeks seek wisdom, but we preach Christ crucified, a stumbling-block to Jews and folly to Gentiles, but to those who are called, both Jews and Greeks, Christ the power of God and the wisdom of God'. This was what Paul had in fact proclaimed when he first came to Corinth from Athens on his second missionary journey, 'I decided to know nothing among you except Jesus Christ and him crucified', and again, 'I delivered to you as of first importance what I also received, that Christ died for our sins in accordance with the scriptures.'[6]

The same emphasis on the cross is to be found in the rest of the New Testament. What Peter thought and wrote about it we shall see later. In the Epistle to the Hebrews comes the unequivocal statement that Christ 'has appeared once for all at the end of the age to put away sin by the sacrifice of himself'. When we reach the mysterious and wonderful book of the Revelation, we catch a glimpse of the glorified Jesus in heaven not only as 'the Lion of the tribe of Judah' but as 'a Lamb standing, as though it had been slain', and we hear the countless multitude of saints and angels singing his praise, 'Worthy is the Lamb who was slain, to receive power and wealth and wisdom and might and honour and glory and blessing!'[7]

So from the early chapters of Genesis to the final chapters of the Revelation we can trace what some writers have called a scarlet thread. It is in fact like the thread of Theseus which enables us to find our way through the labyrinth of Scripture.

[6] Galatians 2:20; 6:14; 1 Corinthians 1:22-24; 2:2; 15:3.
[7] Hebrews 9:26; Revelation 5:5, 6, 12.

And what the Bible teaches concerning the centrality of the cross, the Christian church has recognized. Many churches mark us with the sign of a cross at our baptism and erect a cross over our grave when we are dead. Church buildings have often been constructed on a cruciform ground-plan, with nave and transepts forming a cross, while some Christians wear a cross on lapel, necklace or chain. None of this is accidental. The cross is the symbol of our faith. The Christian faith is 'the faith of Christ crucified'. What the Emperor Constantine is said to have seen in the sky, we can see ourselves in the pages of the Bible: '*In hoc signo vinces.*' There is no conquest without the cross. There is no Christianity without the cross. But why? What does it mean?

The meaning of the cross

I cannot begin to unfold the meaning of the death of Christ without first confessing that much remains a mystery. Christians believe that the cross is the pivotal event in history. Small wonder that our puny minds cannot fully take it in! One day the veil will be altogether removed, and all riddles will be solved. We shall see Christ as he is and worship him through eternity for what he has done. 'Now we see in a mirror dimly, but then face to face. Now I know in part; then I shall understand fully, even as I have been fully understood.' So said the great apostle Paul with his massive intellect and his many revelations; and if he said it, how much more should we?

I shall confine myself to what Simon Peter wrote about the death of Jesus in his first Epistle. I turn to his writings on purpose. I have three reasons.

The first reason is that Peter was one of the inner and intimate group of three apostles. 'Peter, James and John' form a trio who enjoyed a closer fellowship with Jesus than the rest of the Twelve. So Peter is as likely as anyone to have grasped what Jesus thought and taught concerning his death. In fact we find in his first letter several clear reminiscences of his Master's teaching.

Second, I turn to Peter with confidence, because at the beginning he was himself very reluctant to accept the necessity of Christ's sufferings. He had been the first to acknowledge the uniqueness of Christ's person, but he was also the first to deny the need for his death. He who had declared, 'Thou art the Christ' shouted, 'No, Lord' when Jesus began to teach that the Christ must suffer. Throughout the remaining days of Jesus' ministry, Peter retained his dogged hostility to the idea of a Christ who would die. He tried to defend him in the garden, and, when the arrest was a *fait accompli*, followed him at a distance. In sullen disillusionment he denied him three times in the courtyard, and the tears he wept were not only of remorse but of despair. Only after the resurrection, when Jesus taught the apostles from Scripture that it was 'necessary that the Christ should suffer these things and enter into his glory', did Simon Peter at last begin to understand and believe. Within a few weeks he had laid hold of the truth so firmly that he could address the crowd in the Temple cloisters with the words, 'what God foretold by the mouth of all the prophets, that his Christ should suffer, he thus fulfilled', and his first letter contains several references to 'the sufferings and glory of the Christ'. We too may at first be reluctant to admit the necessity of the cross and slow to fathom its meaning, but if anyone can persuade and teach us it will be Simon Peter.

Third, the references to the cross in Peter's first Epistle are asides. If he were deliberately marshalling arguments to prove that the death of Jesus was indispensable, we might suspect him of having some axe to grind. But his allusions are more ethical than doctrinal. He simply urges his readers to live their Christian lives consistently and to bear their sufferings patiently, and then refers them to the cross for their inspiration.

Christ died as our Example

Persecution is the background to this Epistle. The Emperor Nero was known to be hostile to the Christian church, and the hearts of many Christians were failing them for fear. Already spasmodic outbreaks of violence had occurred. It seemed that worse was to come.

The advice Peter gives is straightforward.[8] If Christian servants are ill-treated by pagan masters, let them be sure that they are not receiving a punishment which they deserve. It is no credit to them to accept a beating for wrongdoing. Let them rather suffer for righteousness' sake and welcome reproach for the name of Christ. They are not to resist, still less to retaliate. They must submit. To bear unjust suffering patiently has God's approval. Then at once Peter's mind flies to the cross. Undeserved suffering is part of the Christian's calling, he asserts, 'because Christ also suffered for you, leaving you an example, that you should follow in his steps'. He was sinless and guileless. Yet when he was insulted, he took no revenge; when he suffered, he uttered no threats. He simply committed himself, or as the text may rather read, he committed them (his tormentors) into the hands of the just Judge of all mankind.

Christ has left us an example. The Greek word Peter uses, unique here in the New Testament, denotes a teacher's copybook, the perfect alphabet on which a pupil models his script as he learns to write. So if we would master the ABC of Christian love, we must trace out our lives according to the pattern of Jesus. We must 'follow in his steps'. This verb is eloquent as it comes from Peter's pen. He had boasted that he would follow Jesus to prison and to death, but in the event had 'followed afar off'. Only on the shore of Galilee had Jesus renewed his call and commission to Peter in his familiar terms 'Follow me'. So Peter was urging his readers to join him as he tried now to follow more obediently in the Master's steps.

The challenge of the cross is as uncomfortable in the twentieth century as it was in the first, and is as relevant today as ever it was. Perhaps nothing is more completely opposed to our natural instincts than this command not to resist, but to bear unjust suffering and overcome evil with good. Yet the cross bids us accept injury, love our enemies and leave the outcome to God.

[8] 1 Peter 2:18-25.

The death of Jesus is more than an inspiring example, however. If it were not more than this, much in the story of the Gospels would be inexplicable. There are those strange sayings, for instance, in which he said he would 'give his life as a ransom for many' and shed his blood – 'blood of the covenant', he called it – 'for the forgiveness of sins'.[9] There is no redemption in an example. A pattern cannot secure our pardon.

Besides, why was he burdened with such heavy and anxious foreboding as the cross approached? How shall we explain the dreadful agony in the garden, his tears and cries and bloody sweat? 'My Father, if it be possible, let this cup pass from me; nevertheless, not as I will, but as thou wilt.' Again, 'My Father, if this cannot pass unless I drink it, thy will be done.' Was the cup from which he shrank the symbol of death by crucifixion? Was he then afraid of pain and death? If so, his example may have been one of submission and patience, but it was hardly one of courage. Socrates, Plato tells us, drank his cup of hemlock in the prison cell in Athens 'quite readily and cheerfully'. Was Socrates braver than Jesus? Or were their cups filled with different poison? And what is the meaning of the darkness, and the cry of dereliction, and the rending from top to bottom of the Temple curtain before the Holy of Holies? These things have no explanation if Jesus died only as an example. Indeed some of them would seem to make his example less exemplary.

Not only would much in the Gospels remain mysterious if Christ's death were purely an example, but our human need would remain unsatisfied. We need more than an example; we need a Saviour. An example can stir our imagination, kindle our idealism and strengthen our resolve, but it cannot cleanse the defilement of our past sins, bring peace to our troubled conscience or reconcile us to God.

In any case, the apostles leave us in no doubt about the matter. They regularly associate Christ's coming and death with our *sins*.

[9] Mark 10:45; Matthew 26:28.

'Christ died for our sins in accordance with the scriptures.'

'Christ also died for sins once for all.'

'You know that he appeared to take away sins.'

Here are the three great apostolic writers of the New Testament, Paul, Peter and John, unanimous in linking his death with our sins.[10]

Christ died as our Sinbearer

The phrase which Peter uses in his letter (2:24) to describe the relation between Christ's death and our sins is this: 'he himself bore our sins in his body on the tree'. The expression to 'bear sin' has a rather foreign sound in our ears, and we shall need to go back to the Old Testament to understand it. The idea occurs frequently in the books of Leviticus and Numbers. Many times it is written of an offender who infringes one of God's revealed laws that 'he shall bear his iniquity' or 'he shall bear his sin'. For instance, 'If any one sins, doing any of the things which the Lord has commanded not to be done . . . he is guilty and shall bear his iniquity'.[11] The expression can only mean one thing. To 'bear sin' is to suffer the consequences of one's sin, to bear its penalty.

But at times it is implied that somebody else can assume responsibility for the sinner. In the thirtieth chapter of the book Numbers, which deals with the validity of vows, Moses explains that a vow taken by a man or a widow must stand. A vow, however, taken by an unmarried girl or by a married woman must be validated by her father and her husband respectively. If on the day on which the man hears of the woman's vow he does not invalidate it, and it later proves to be foolish, it is said, '*he* shall bear *her* iniquity'. Another example comes towards the end of the Book of Lamentations, in which after the destruction of Jerusalem the Israelites cry: 'Our fathers sinned, and are no more; and *we* bear *their* iniquities.'

This possibility of somebody else accepting the responsibility for, and bearing the consequences of, our sins was further

10 1 Corinthians 15:3; 1 Peter 3:18; 1 John 3:5.
11 Leviticus 5:17.

taught by those Old Testament blood sacrifices in the Mosaic legislation which seem so strange to us today. Of the sin offering it was said that God had given it to 'bear the iniquity of the congregation, to make atonement for them before the Lord'. Similarly, on the annual Day of Atonement, Aaron was instructed to lay his hands on the head of the scapegoat, thus identifying himself and his people with it; he was then to confess the nation's sins, symbolically transferring them to the goat, which was driven out into the wilderness; and next we read, 'The goat shall bear all their iniquities upon him to a solitary land'.[12] It is plain from this that to 'bear' somebody else's sin is to become his substitute, to bear the penalty of his sin in his place.

Despite this remarkable temporary provision, 'it is impossible that the blood of bulls and goats should take away sins', as the writer to the Hebrews says. So in the longest Servant Song of Isaiah (chapter 53), the innocent sufferer (who foreshadows Christ) is described in terms which are intentionally sacrificial. He was 'like a lamb that is led to the slaughter' both because 'he opened not his mouth' and because 'the Lord has laid on him the iniquity of us all', so that his soul was made 'an offering for sin'. We all 'like sheep have gone astray', but he also 'like a sheep' 'was wounded for our transgressions, he was bruised for our iniquities; upon him was the chastisement that made us whole, and with his stripes we are healed'. Now all this clear language of substitution, describing him as 'stricken for the transgression of my people', is summed up in the chapter in the two phrases with which we have been made familiar by Leviticus, 'he shall bear their iniquities' and 'he bore the sin of many'.

When at last after centuries of preparation Jesus Christ himself arrived, John the Baptist greeted him publicly with the extraordinary words: 'Behold, the Lamb of God, who takes away the sin of the world!' Similarly, when later the New Testament came to be written, its authors have no difficulty in recognizing the death of Jesus as the final sacrifice in which all

[12] Leviticus 10:17, AV; 16:22.

the Old Testament sacrifices were fulfilled. This truth is an important part of the message of the Epistle to the Hebrews. The old sacrifices were of bulls and goats: Christ offered himself. The old sacrifices were interminably repeated: Christ died once and for all. He was 'offered once to bear the sins of many'.

This last phrase brings us back to Peter's expression, 'he himself bore our sins in his body on the tree'. The Son of God identified himself with the sins of men. He was not content to take our nature upon him; he took our iniquity upon him as well. He was not only 'made flesh' in the womb of Mary; he was 'made sin' on the cross of Calvary.

These last words are Paul's. They are among the most startling in the whole biblical teaching about the atonement. But we cannot escape their significance. In the previous verses (in 2 Corinthians 5) Paul has affirmed that God refused to impute our sins to us, or count them against us. That is, in his utterly undeserved love for us, he would not make us answerable for our sins. He would not allow it to be said of us as it was of so many in Old Testament days, 'they shall bear their iniquity'. Then what did he do? 'For our sake he made him to be sin who knew no sin, so that in him we might become the righteousness of God.' Jesus Christ had no sins of his own; he was made sin with our sins, on the cross.

As we look at the cross, we can begin to understand the terrible implications of these words. At twelve noon 'there was darkness over the whole land' which continued for three hours until Jesus died. With the darkness came silence, for no eye should see, and no lips could tell, the agony of soul which the spotless Lamb of God now endured. The accumulated sins of all human history were laid upon him. Voluntarily he bore them in his own body. He made them his own. He shouldered full responsibility for them.

And then in desolate spiritual abandonment that cry was wrung from his lips, 'My God, my God, why hast thou forsaken me?' It was a quotation from the first verse of Psalm 22. No doubt he had been meditating during his agony on its description of the sufferings and glory of the Christ. But why

92

did he quote that verse? Why not one of the triumphant verses at the end? Why not, 'You who fear the Lord, praise him!' or 'Dominion belongs to the Lord'? Are we to believe that it was a cry of human weakness and despair, or that the Son of God was imagining things?

No. These words must be taken at their face value. He quoted this verse of Scripture, as he quoted all others, because he believed he was himself fulfilling it. He was bearing our sins. And God who is 'of purer eyes than to behold evil' and cannot 'look on wrong' turned away his face. Our sins came between the Father and the Son. The Lord Jesus Christ who was eternally with the Father, who enjoyed unbroken communion with him throughout his life on earth, was thus momentarily abandoned. Our sins sent Christ to hell. He tasted the torment of a soul estranged from God. Bearing our sins, he died our death. He endured instead of us the penalty of separation from God which our sins deserved.

Then at once, emerging from that outer darkness, he cried in triumph, 'It is finished', and finally, 'Father, into thy hands I commit my spirit'. And so he died. The work he had come to do was completed. The salvation he had come to win was accomplished. The sins of the world were borne. Reconciliation to God was available to all who would trust this Saviour for themselves, and receive him as their own. Immediately, as if to demonstrate this truth publicly, the unseen hand of God tore down the curtain of the Temple, and hurled it aside. It was needed no longer. The way into God's holy presence was no longer barred. Christ had 'opened the gate of heaven to all believers'. And thirty-six hours later he was raised from death, to prove that he had not died in vain.

This simple and wonderful tale of the sinbearing of the Son of God is strangely unpopular today. That he should have borne our sins and taken our penalty is said to be immoral or unworthy or unjust. And of course it can easily be travestied. We are not suggesting that there is nothing left for us to do. Of course we must return 'to the Shepherd and Guardian of our souls', dying to sin and living to righteousness, as Peter went on to say. Above all we do not forget that 'all this is from God', issuing from his unimaginable mercy. We are not to think of Jesus Christ as a third party wresting salvation for us from a God unwilling to save. No. The initiative was with God himself. 'God was in Christ reconciling the world unto himself.' Precisely *how* he can have been in Christ while he made Christ to be sin for us, I cannot explain, but the same apostle states both truths in the same paragraph. And we must accept this paradox along with the equally baffling paradox that Jesus of Nazareth was both God and Man, and yet one person. If there was a paradox in his person, it is not surprising that we find one in his work as well.

But even if we cannot resolve the paradox or fathom the mystery, we should believe the direct statement of Christ and his apostles, that he bore our sins, understanding the phrase in its biblical meaning that he underwent the penalty of our sins for us.

That Peter meant this is clear from three considerations. First, he says that it was on the 'tree' that Christ bore our sins. There can be no doubt he used the word deliberately, just as he did in his early sermons recorded in the Acts, for instance when he said, 'The God of our fathers raised Jesus whom you killed by hanging him on a tree'. His Jewish listeners would have had no difficulty in grasping his implied reference to Deuteronomy 23, where it was written, 'Cursed be every one who hangs on a tree'. The fact that Jesus ended his life hanging on a 'tree' (for the Jews regarded nailing to a cross and hanging on a tree as equivalents) meant that he was under the divine curse.

Instead of repudiating this idea, the apostles accepted it, and Paul explained it in Galatians 3. He pointed out that it was also written in Deuteronomy: 'Cursed be every one who does not abide by all things written in the book of the law, and do them.' But then 'Christ redeemed us from the curse of the law, having become a curse for us – for it is written, "Cursed be every one who hangs on a tree".' The meaning of these verses in the context is plain and inescapable. It is this: the righteous curse of the broken law which rests on transgressors was transferred to Jesus on the cross. He has freed us from the curse by taking it upon himself when he died.

Second, this passage in Peter's first letter contains no fewer than five clear verbal reminiscences of Isaiah 53:

I PETER 2	ISAIAH 53
He committed no sin; no guile was found on his lips	He had done no violence, and there was no deceit in his mouth
He was reviled	He was despised and rejected by men
He himself bore our sins	He bore the sin of many
By his wounds you have been healed	With his stripes we are healed
You were straying like sheep	All we like sheep have gone astray

We have already seen that this chapter portrays an innocent sufferer who in a sacrificial death is wounded for the transgressions of others. It is beyond question that Jesus himself interpreted his mission and death in the light of this chapter, as did his followers after him. For example, when the Ethiopian eunuch asked the evangelist Philip to whom the prophet was referring in this passage which he was reading in his chariot, Philip immediately 'told him the good news of Jesus'.

Third, Peter has other references to the cross in his letter which confirm our interpretation of his words in the second chapter. He describes his readers as having been 'ransomed . . . with the precious blood of Christ, like that of a lamb without blemish or spot', and even as having been 'sprinkled' with his blood.[13] Both expressions allude to the original Passover sacrifice at the time of the Exodus. Each Israelite family took a lamb, killed it, and sprinkled its blood on the lintel and side posts of the house. Only so were they safe from the judgment of God and only so did they escape from the slavery of Egypt. Peter boldly applies the Passover symbolism to Christ (as does

[13] 1 Peter 1:2, 18, 19.

Paul also, 'Christ, our paschal lamb, has been sacrificed'). His blood was shed to redeem us from the judgment of God and the bondage of sin. If we are to benefit from it, it must be sprinkled on our hearts, that is, applied to each of us individually.

Peter's other significant reference to the cross is in 3:18: 'Christ also died for sins once for all, the righteous for the unrighteous, that he might bring us to God. . . .' Sin had separated us from God; but Christ desired to bring us back to God. So he suffered for our sins, an innocent Saviour dying for guilty sinners. And he did it 'once for all', decisively, so that what he did cannot be repeated or improved upon or even supplemented.

We must not miss the implication of this. It means that no religious observances or good deeds of ours could ever earn our forgiveness. Yet a great many people in the post-Christian west have fallen for this caricature of Christianity. They then understandably see no fundamental difference between the Christian gospel and the eastern religions. For they regard all religion as a system of human merit. 'God helps those who help themselves', they say. But there is no possibility of reconciling this notion with the cross of Christ. He died to atone for our sins for the simple reason that we cannot atone for them ourselves. If we could, his atoning death would be redundant. Indeed, to claim that we can secure God's favour by our own efforts is an insult to Jesus Christ. For it is tantamount to saying that we can manage without him; he really need not have bothered to die. As Paul put it, 'if justification (*i.e.* acceptance with God) were through the law (*i.e.* through our obedience), then Christ died to no purpose'.[14]

The message of the cross remains, in our day as in Paul's, folly to the wise and a stumbling-block to the self-righteous, but it has brought peace to the conscience of millions. As Richard Hooker wrote in a sermon which he preached in 1585 when he was Master of the Temple,

'Let it be accounted folly, or frenzy, or fury, or whatsoever. It is our wisdom and our comfort; we care for no knowledge in the world

14 Galatians 2:21.

but this, that man hath sinned and God hath suffered; that God hath made himself the sin of men, and that men are made the righteousness of God.'

Every Christian can echo these words. There is healing through his wounds, life through his death, pardon through his pain, salvation through his suffering.

8 THE SALVATION OF CHRIST

'Salvation' is a wonderfully comprehensive term. It is a great mistake to suppose that it is merely a synonym for forgiveness. God is as much concerned with our present and future as with our past. His plan is first to reconcile us to himself, and then progressively to liberate us from our self-centredness and bring us into harmony with our fellow men. We owe our forgiveness and reconciliation chiefly to the death of Christ, but it is by his Spirit that we can be set free from ourselves and in his church that we can be united in a fellowship of love. These are the aspects of Christ's salvation which we must now consider.

The spirit of Christ

As we have seen, our sins should not be viewed as a series of unrelated incidents, but as the symptoms of an inward moral disease. To illustrate this, Jesus several times used the simile of the tree and the fruit. The quality of fruits, he taught, depends on the quality of the tree which bears them. 'Every sound tree bears good fruit, but the bad tree bears evil fruit. A sound tree cannot bear evil fruit, nor can a bad tree bear good fruit.'

The cause of our sins, therefore, is our sin, our inherited nature which is perverted and self-centred. As Jesus put it, our sins come from within, out of our 'heart'. Therefore an improvement in behaviour depends on a change of nature. 'Make the tree good', said Jesus, 'and its fruit (will be) good.'

But can human nature be changed? Is it possible to make a

sour person sweet, a proud person humble, or a selfish person unselfish? The Bible declares emphatically that these miracles can take place. It is part of the glory of the gospel. Jesus Christ offers to change not only our standing before God but our very nature. He spoke to Nicodemus of the indispensable necessity of a new birth, and his words are still applicable to us: 'Truly, truly, I say to you, unless one is born anew, he cannot see the kingdom of God . . . Do not marvel that I said to you, "You must be born anew".'[1]

Paul's statement is in some ways even more dramatic, for he blurts out, in a sentence which has no verbs: 'If anyone in Christ – new creation!'[2] Here then is the possibility of which the New Testament speaks – a new heart, a new nature, a new birth, a new creation.

This tremendous inward change is the work of the Holy Spirit. The new birth is a birth 'from above'. To be born again is to be 'born of the Spirit'. It is hardly relevant here to discuss the mysterious doctrine of the Trinity. For our present purpose it is sufficient to consider what the apostles wrote about the Holy Spirit as their teaching was illumined by their experience.

First, however, it is important to realize that the Holy Spirit neither came into existence, nor began to be active, at Pentecost. He is God. He is therefore eternal and has been at work in the world since the creation. The Old Testament contains many references to him, and the prophets looked forward to the time when his activity would increase and spread, when God would put his Spirit within his people, and so enable them to obey his law.

What the Old Testament prophets foretold, Christ promised as an immediate expectation. A few hours before he died, secluded in the upper room with the apostles, he spoke of 'the Comforter', 'the Spirit of truth', who would come and take his place.

Indeed, the Holy Spirit's presence would be better for them even than his own earthly presence had been. 'It is to your

[1] See John 3.
[2] 2 Corinthians 5:17, literally.

99

advantage that I go away,' he said, 'for if I do not go away, the Counsellor will not come to you; but if I go, I will send him to you.' The advantage was mainly this. Christ had only been *with* them, at their side; but 'he . . . will be *in* you'.[3]

There is a sense in which we may say that the teaching ministry of Jesus had proved a failure. Several times he had urged his disciples to humble themselves like a little child, but Simon Peter remained proud and self-confident. Often he had told them to love one another, but even John seems to have deserved his nickname 'son of thunder' to the end. Yet when you read Peter's first letter you cannot fail to notice its references to humility, and John's letters are full of love. What made the difference? The Holy Spirit. Jesus taught them to be humble and loving; but neither quality appeared in their lives until the Holy Spirit entered their personality and began to change them from within.

On the Day of Pentecost 'they were all filled with the Holy Spirit'. Do not imagine that this was a freak experience for apostles and other eminent saints, although doubtless we are not to expect a repetition of the outward phenomena like the rushing wind and tongues of fire. 'Be filled with the Spirit' is a command addressed to all Christians. The inner presence of the Holy Spirit is the spiritual birthright of every Christian. Indeed, if the Holy Spirit has not taken up residence within us, we are not real Christians at all. 'Any one who does not have the Spirit of Christ does not belong to him,' Paul wrote.[4]

This then is what the New Testament teaches. When we put our trust in Jesus Christ and commit ourselves to him, the Holy Spirit enters us. He is sent by God 'into our hearts'. He makes our bodies his temple.[5]

This does not mean that from now on we are exempt from the possibility of sinning. On the contrary, in some ways the conflict is intensified; but on the other hand, a way of victory has been opened. Paul gives a vivid description of the battle in

[3] See John 16:7; 14:17.

[4] See Acts 2:4; Ephesians 5:18; Romans 8:9.

[5] Galatians 4:6; 1 Corinthians 6:19.

the fifth chapter of his letter to the Galatians. The combatants are 'the flesh', his name for our inherited self-centred nature, and 'the Spirit'. 'The desires of the flesh', he explains, 'are against the Spirit, and the desires of the Spirit are against the flesh; for these are opposed to each other.'

This is not arid theological theorizing; it is the daily experience of every Christian. We continue to be conscious of sinful desires which are tugging us down; but we are now also aware of a counteracting force pulling us upwards to holiness. If 'the flesh' were given free rein, it would stampede us into the jungle of immoral and selfish vices which Paul lists in verses 19 to 21. If, on the other hand, the Holy Spirit is allowed his way, the result will be 'love, joy, peace, patience, kindness, goodness, faithfulness, gentleness, self-control'. These attractive virtues Paul names 'the fruit of the Spirit'. Our human character is likened to an orchard which the Holy Spirit is cultivating. Let him make the trees good, and their fruit will be good also.

How then can 'the flesh' be subdued, so that 'the fruit of the Spirit' may grow and ripen? The answer lies in the inner attitude which we adopt towards each. 'Those who belong to Christ Jesus have crucified the flesh with its passions and desires.' 'Walk by (or, in) the Spirit, and do not (or, you will not) gratify the desires of the flesh.' Towards 'the flesh' we must take up such an attitude of fierce resistance and ruthless rejection that only the word 'crucifixion' can describe it; but to the indwelling Spirit we must trustfully surrender the undisputed dominion over our lives. The more we make a habit of denying the flesh and obeying the Spirit, the more the ugly works of the flesh will disappear and the lovely fruit of the Spirit will take their place.

Paul teaches the same truth in 2 Corinthians 3:18: 'We all, with unveiled face, beholding the glory of the Lord, are being changed into his likeness from one degree of glory to another; for this comes from the Lord who is the Spirit.' It is by the Spirit of Christ that we can be transformed into the image of Christ, as we keep looking steadfastly towards him. We thus have our part to play, in repentance, faith and discipline, but essentially holiness is the work of the Holy Spirit.

> And every virtue we possess
> And every victory won,
> And every thought of holiness,
> Are his alone.

> Spirit of purity and grace,
> Our weakness, pitying, see;
> O make our hearts thy dwelling-place,
> And worthier thee!

William Temple used to illustrate the point in this way. It is no good giving me a play like Hamlet or King Lear, and telling me to write a play like that. Shakespeare could do it; I can't. And it is no good showing me a life like the life of Jesus and telling me to live a life like that. Jesus could do it; I can't. But if the genius of Shakespeare could come and live in me, then I could write plays like that. And if the Spirit of Jesus could come and live in me, then I could live a life like that. This is the secret of Christian sanctity. It is not that we should strive to live like Jesus, but that he by his Spirit should come and live in us. To have him as our example is not enough; we need him as our Saviour.

It is thus through his atoning death that the penalty of our sins may be forgiven; it is through his indwelling Spirit that the power of our sins may be broken.

The church of Christ

The tendency of sin is centrifugal. It pulls us out of harmony with our neighbours. It estranges us not only from our Maker but from our fellow-creatures too. We all know from experience how a community, whether a college, a hospital, a factory or an office, can become a hotbed of jealousy and animosity. We find it very difficult 'to dwell together in unity'.

But God's plan is to reconcile us to each other as well as to himself. So he does not save independent, unconnected individuals in isolation from one another; he is calling out *a people* for his own possession.

Already in the early chapters of Genesis this is made clear. God called Abraham to leave his home and relations in Mesopotamia, and promised to give him both a land for his inheritance and descendants as numerous as the stars in the sky and the sand on the seashore. This pledge to multiply Abraham's posterity and through them to bless all the nations of the earth was renewed to his son Isaac and his grandson Jacob.

Jacob, however, died in exile in Egypt. But his twelve sons survived him and became the fathers of the twelve tribes of 'Israel', the name God had given to Jacob. With these 'children of Israel', rescued years later from their Egyptian slavery, God renewed his covenant.

But how were all the families of the earth to be blessed? Century followed century, as the fortunes of Israel unfolded, and still the nation seemed to the rest of the world more a curse than a blessing. Surrounded by high walls of their own building, God's people protected themselves from defiling contact with the unclean Gentiles. It seemed as if they would miss their destiny as benefactors of the world. Was God's promise to Abraham to prove a lie? No. Many of the prophets knew by the word of the Lord that when the Messiah came, God's own anointed Prince, pilgrims would come from every point of the compass to enter the kingdom of God.

At last the Christ came. Jesus of Nazareth announced the arrival of the long-awaited kingdom. Many would come, he said, from north, south, east and west, and sit down with Abraham, Isaac and Jacob. God's people would no longer be a nation apart, but a society whose members would be drawn from every race, kindred and language. 'Go . . .', the risen Lord commanded his followers, 'and make disciples of all nations . . .'. The sum total of these disciples he called 'my church'.[6]

So God's pledge to Abraham, repeated several times to him and renewed to his sons, is being fulfilled in the growth of the world-wide church today. 'If you are Christ's,' wrote Paul, 'then you are Abraham's offspring, heirs according to promise.'[7]

[6] Matthew 28:19; 16:18.
[7] Galatians 3:29.

One of the most striking pictures which Paul uses to convey the unity of believers in Christ is that of the human body. The church, he says, is the body of Christ. Every Christian is a member or organ of the body, while Christ himself is the head, controlling the body's activities. Not every organ has the same function, but each is necessary for the maximum health and usefulness of the body.

The whole body is also animated by a common life. This is the Holy Spirit. It is his presence which makes the body one. The church owes its coherent unity to him. 'There is one body and one Spirit', emphasizes Paul. Even the outward, organizational divisions of the church, regrettable as they are, do not destroy its inward and spiritual unity. This is indissoluble, for it is 'the unity of the Spirit' or 'the fellowship of the Spirit'.[8] Our common share in him makes us deeply and permanently one.

It is nonsense of course to claim membership of a great world-wide body, the church universal, without in practice sharing in one of its local manifestations. It is here, as members of a local church, that we shall find opportunities to worship God, to enjoy fellowship with one another and to serve the wider community.

Many today react against the church as an organization, and some entirely reject it. This is often understandable, for the church can certainly be archaic, inward-looking and reactionary. We must remember, however, that the church is people – sinful and fallible people. This is no reason to shun it, for we are sinful and fallible ourselves.

We have also to recognize that not all members of the visible church are necessarily members of the real church of Jesus Christ. Some whose names are inscribed on church rolls and registers have never had their names, as Jesus put it, 'written in heaven'. Although this is a fact to which the Bible often refers, yet it is not for us to judge: 'the Lord knows those who are his'. The minister by baptism welcomes into the visible church those who *profess* faith in Christ. But only God knows

[8] Ephesians 4:3, 4; Philippians 2:1; 2 Corinthians 13:14.

those who actually *exercise* faith, for only God sees the heart. No doubt the two companies largely overlap. They are not, however, identical.

The Holy Spirit is not only the author of the common life of the church, but the creator of its common love as well. The first-fruit of the Spirit is love. His very nature is love, and imparts it to those whom he indwells. All Christians have known the remarkable experience of being drawn to other Christians whom they hardly know and whose background may be very different from their own. The relationship which exists and grows between the children of God is deeper and sweeter even than blood relationships. It is the kinship of the family of God. Truly 'we know that we have passed out of death into life, because we love the brethren', as John says. This love is not sentimental. It is not even fundamentally emotional. Its essence is self-sacrifice; it manifests itself in the desire to serve, help and enrich others. It is by love that the centrifugal force of sin is counteracted, for sin divides where love unites, and sin separates where love reconciles.

Of course the pages of the church's history have often been smudged by stupidity and selfishness, even by open disobedience to the teaching of Christ. Still today some churches appear to be dead or dying, rather than vibrant with life; and others are torn by factions and blighted by lovelessness. We have to admit that not all those who profess and call themselves Christians exhibit either the love or the life of Jesus Christ.

Nevertheless the Christian's place is in the local Christian community, however imperfect it may be, there to seek the new quality of relationship which Christ gives his people, and in that fellowship to share in the church's worship and witness.

Part Four: Man's Response

9 COUNTING THE COST

So far we have examined some of the evidence for the unique deity of Jesus of Nazareth; we have considered man's need as a sinner, estranged from God, imprisoned in himself and out of harmony with his fellows; and we have outlined the main aspects of the salvation which Christ has won for us, and offers to us. It is now time for us to ask the personal question put to Jesus Christ by Saul of Tarsus on the Damascus road, 'What shall I do, Lord?' or the similar question asked by the Philippian jailor, 'What must I do to be saved?'

Clearly we must do something. Christianity is no mere passive acquiescence in a series of propositions, however true. We may believe in the deity and the salvation of Christ, and acknowledge ourselves to be sinners in need of his salvation; but this does not make us Christians. We have to make a personal response to Jesus Christ, committing ourselves unreservedly to him as our Saviour and Lord. The precise nature of this step we shall leave to the next chapter; some of its practical implications will concern us in this.

Jesus never concealed the fact that his religion included a demand as well as an offer. Indeed, the demand was as total as the offer was free. If he offered men his salvation, he also demanded their submission. He gave no encouragement whatever to thoughtless applicants for discipleship. He brought no pressure to bear on any enquirer. He sent irresponsible enthusiasts empty away. Luke tells us of three men who either volunteered, or were invited, to follow Jesus; but not one passed the Lord's tests. The rich young ruler, too, moral, earnest and attractive, who wanted eternal life on his own terms, went away sorrowful, with his riches intact but with neither life nor Christ as his possession.

On another occasion great crowds were following Jesus. Perhaps they were shouting their slogans of allegiance and giving an impressive outward demonstration of their loyalty. But Jesus knew how superficial their attachment to him was. Stopping, and turning round to speak to them, he told a pointed parable in the form of a question:

> 'Which of you, desiring to build a tower, does not first sit down and count the cost, whether he has enough to complete it? Otherwise, when he has laid a foundation, and is not able to finish, all who see it begin to mock him, saying, "This man began to build, and was not able to finish".'[1]

The Christian landscape is strewn with the wreckage of derelict, half-built towers – the ruins of those who began to build and were unable to finish. For thousands of people still ignore Christ's warning and undertake to follow him without first pausing to reflect on the cost of doing so. The result is the great scandal of Christendom today, so-called 'nominal Christianity'. In countries to which Christian civilization has spread, large numbers of people have covered themselves with a decent, but thin, veneer of Christianity. They have allowed themselves to become somewhat involved; enough to be respectable but not enough to be uncomfortable. Their religion is a great, soft cushion. It protects them from the hard unpleasantness of life, while changing its place and shape to suit their convenience. No wonder the cynics speak of hypocrites in the church and dismiss religion as escapism.

The message of Jesus was very different. He never lowered his standards or modified his conditions to make his call more readily acceptable. He asked his first disciples, and he has asked every disciple since, to give him their thoughtful and total commitment. Nothing less than this will do.

We are now in a position to discuss precisely what he said.

'He called to him the multitude with his disciples, and said to them,
[1] Luke 14:25-30.

"If any man would come after me, let him deny himself and take up his cross and follow me. For whoever would save his life will lose it; and whoever loses his life for my sake and the gospel's will save it. For what does it profit a man, to gain the whole world and forfeit his life? For what can a man give in return for his life? For whoever is ashamed of me and of my words in this adulterous and sinful generation, of him will the Son of man also be ashamed, when he comes in the glory of his Father with the holy angels." [2]

The call to follow Christ

At its simplest Christ's call was 'Follow me'. He asked men and women for their personal allegiance. He invited them to learn from him, to obey his words and to identify themselves with his cause.

Now there can be no following without a previous forsaking. To follow Christ is to renounce all lesser loyalties. In the days when he lived among men on earth, this meant a literal abandonment of home and work. Simon and Andrew 'left their nets and followed him'. James and John 'left their father Zebedee in the boat with the hired servants, and followed him'. Matthew, who heard Christ's call while he was 'sitting at the tax office . . . left everything, and rose and followed him'.

Today, in principle, the call of the Lord Jesus has not changed. He still says 'Follow me', and adds, 'whoever of you does not renounce all that he has cannot be my disciple'. In practice, however, this does not mean for the majority of Christians a physical departure from their home or their job. It implies rather an inner surrender of both, and a refusal to allow either family or ambition to occupy the first place in our lives.

Let me be more explicit about the forsaking which cannot be separated from the following of Jesus Christ.

First, there must be *a renunciation of sin*. This, in a word, is repentance. It is the first part of Christian conversion. It can in no circumstances be bypassed. Repentance and faith belong together. We cannot follow Christ without forsaking sin.

[2] Mark 8:34-38.

Repentance is a definite turn from every thought, word, deed and habit which is known to be wrong. It is not sufficient to feel pangs of remorse or to make some kind of apology to God. Fundamentally, repentance is a matter neither of emotion nor of speech. It is an inward change of mind and attitude towards sin which leads to a change of behaviour.

There can be no compromise here. There may be sins in our lives which we do not think we ever could renounce; but we must be *willing* to let them go as we cry to God for deliverance from them. If you are in doubt regarding what is right and what wrong, what must go and what may be retained, do not be too greatly influenced by the customs and conventions of Christians you may know. Go by the clear teaching of the Bible and by the prompting of your conscience, and Christ will gradually lead you further along the path of righteousness. When he puts his finger on anything, give it up. It may be some association or recreation, some literature we read, or some attitude of pride, jealousy or resentment, or an unforgiving spirit.

Jesus told his followers to pluck out their eye and cut off their hand or foot if these caused them to sin. We are not to obey this with dead literalism, of course, and mutilate our bodies. It is a vivid figure of speech for dealing ruthlessly with the avenues along which temptation comes to us.

Sometimes, true repentance has to include 'restitution'. This means putting things right with other people, whom we may have injured. All our sins wound God, and nothing we do can heal the wound. Only the atoning death of our Saviour, Jesus Christ, can do this. But when our sins have damaged other people, we can sometimes help to repair the damage, and where we can, we must. Zacchaeus, the dishonest tax-collector, more than repaid the money he had stolen from his clients and promised to give away half his capital to the poor to compensate (no doubt) for thefts he could not make good. We must follow his example. There may be money or time for us to pay back, rumours to be contradicted, property to return, apologies to be made, or broken relationships to be mended.

We must not be excessively over-scrupulous in this matter, however. It would be foolish to rummage through past years and make an issue of insignificant words or deeds long ago forgotten by the offended person. Nevertheless, we must be realistic about this duty. I have known a student rightly confess to the university authorities that she had cheated in an exam, and another return text-books which he had lifted from a shop. An army officer sent to the War Department a list of items he had 'scrounged'. If we really repent, we shall want to do everything in our power to redress the past. We cannot continue to enjoy the fruits of the sins we want to be forgiven.

Second, there must be *a renunciation of self*. In order to follow Christ we must not only forsake isolated sins, but renounce the very principle of self-will which lies at the root of every act of sin. To follow Christ is to surrender to him the rights over our own lives. It is to abdicate the throne of our heart and do homage to him as our King. This renunciation of self is vividly described by Jesus in three phrases.

It is to *deny ourselves*: 'If any man would come after me, let him deny himself.' The same verb is used of Peter's denial of the Lord in the courtyard of the high priest's palace. We are to disown ourselves as completely as Peter disowned Christ when he said 'I do not know the man'. Self-denial is not just giving up sweets and cigarettes, either for good or for a period of voluntary abstinence. For it is not to deny things to myself, but to deny myself to myself. It is to say no to self, and yes to Christ; to repudiate self and acknowledge Christ.

The next phrase Jesus used is to *take up the cross*: 'If any man would come after me, let him deny himself and take up his cross and follow me.' If we had lived in Palestine and seen a man carrying his cross, we should at once have recognized him as a convicted prisoner being led out to pay the supreme penalty. For Palestine was an occupied country, and this is what the Romans compelled their convicted criminals to do. So, writes Professor H. B. Swete in his commentary on Mark's Gospel, to take up the cross is 'to put oneself into the position of a condemned man on his way to execution'. In other words, the attitude to self which we are to adopt is that of crucifixion. Paul uses the same metaphor when he declares that 'those who belong to Christ Jesus have crucified the flesh (*i.e.* their fallen nature) with its passions and desires'.

In Luke's version of this saying of Christ the adverb 'daily' is added. Every day the Christian is to die. Every day he renounces the sovereignty of his own will. Every day he renews his unconditional surrender to Jesus Christ.

The third expression which Jesus used to describe the renunciation of self is to *lose our life*: 'Whoever loses his life . . . will save it.' The word for 'life' here denotes neither our physical existence nor our soul, but our self. The *psyche* is the ego, the human personality which thinks, feels, plans and chooses. According to a similar saying preserved by Luke Jesus simply used the reflexive pronoun and talked about a man forfeiting 'himself'. The man who commits himself to Christ, therefore, loses himself. This does not mean that he loses his individuality, however. His will is indeed submitted to Christ's will, but his personality is not absorbed into Christ's personality. On the contrary, as we shall see later, when the Christian loses himself, he finds himself, he discovers his true identity.

So in order to follow Christ we have to deny ourselves, to crucify ourselves, to lose ourselves. The full, inexorable demand of Jesus Christ is now laid bare. He does not call us to a sloppy half-heartedness, but to a vigorous, absolute commitment. He calls us to make him our Lord.

The astonishing idea is current in some circles today that we can enjoy the benefits of Christ's salvation without accepting the challenge of his sovereign lordship. Such an unbalanced notion is not to be found in the New Testament. 'Jesus is Lord' is the earliest known formulation of the creed of Christians. In days when imperial Rome was pressing its citizens to say 'Caesar is Lord', these words had a dangerous flavour. But Christians did not flinch. They could not give Caesar their first allegiance, because they had already given it to the Emperor Jesus. God had exalted his Son Jesus far above all principality and power and invested him with a rank superior to every rank, that before him 'every knee should bow . . . and every tongue confess that Jesus Christ is Lord'.[3]

To make Christ Lord is to bring every department of our public and private lives under his control. This includes our career. God has a purpose for every life. Our business is to discover it and do it. God's plan may be different from our parents' or our own. If he is wise, the Christian will do nothing rash or reckless. He may already be engaged in, or preparing for, the work God has for him to do. But he may not. If Christ is our Lord, we must open our minds to the possibility of a change.

What is certain is that God calls every Christian to 'ministry', that is, to service, to be the servant of other people for the sake of Christ. No Christian can live for himself any longer. What is not certain is what form this service will take. It might be the ordained ministry of the church, or some other kind of full-time church work at home or overseas. But it is a great mistake to suppose that every committed Christian is called to this. There are other forms of service which equally deserve the job description 'Christian ministry'. For example, the calling of many girls to be wife, mother and home-maker is in the fullest sense 'Christian ministry', since she is serving Christ, her family and the community. So is every form of work – medicine, research, the law, education, social service, central and local government, industry, business and trade – in which the worker sees himself as cooperating with God in the service of man.

Do not be in too great a hurry to discover God's will for your life. If you are surrendered to it and waiting on God to disclose it, he will make it known to you in his own time. Whatever it proves to be, the Christian cannot be idle. Whether he is an employer, an employee or self-employed, he has a heavenly Master. He learns to grasp God's purpose in his work, and labours at it with all his heart, 'as serving the Lord and not men'.

[3] Philippians 2:10, 11.

Another department of life which passes under the lordship of Jesus Christ is our marriage and our home. Jesus once said, 'Do not think that I have come to bring peace on earth; I have not come to bring peace, but a sword.' He went on to speak of the clash of loyalties which sometimes arises within a family when one of its members begins to follow him.

Such family conflicts still take place today. The Christian should never seek them. He has a definite duty to love and honour his parents and other members of his family. Since he is called to be a peacemaker, he will make as many concessions as he can without compromising his duty to God. Yet he can never forget Christ's word: 'He who loves father or mother... son or daughter more than me is not worthy of me.'[4]

Further, a Christian is at liberty to marry only a Christian. The Bible is definite here: 'do not be mismated with unbelievers'.[5] This command can bring great distress to somebody who is already engaged or nearly so, but the fact must be honestly faced. Marriage is not merely a convenient social custom. It is a divine institution. And the married relationship is the deepest into which human beings can enter. God designed it to be an intimate union, not only physical, emotional, intellectual and social, but spiritual. For a Christian to marry someone with whom he or she cannot be spiritually one is not only to disobey God but to miss the fullness of the union he intended. It also puts the children of the marriage at risk, for it introduces them to religious conflict in their own home and makes impossible the Christian education they should receive from both their parents.

Indeed, so radical is Christian conversion that our whole attitude to marriage, and to relations between the sexes, is likely to change. We begin to see sexuality – the fundamental distinction between man and woman, and the need of each for the other – as itself the creation of God. And sex – the physical expression of sexuality—is no longer debased by selfish

[4] Matthew 10:34, 37.
[5] 2 Corinthians 6:14.

irresponsibility into something casual and essentially impersonal, but becomes what the Creator meant it to be, something good and right, the expression of love, a fulfilment of the divine purpose and of the human personality.

Other formerly private affairs over which Jesus Christ becomes Master, when we commit our lives to him, are our money and our time. Jesus often spoke about money, and about the danger of riches. Much of his teaching on the subject is very disturbing. It sometimes seems as if he was recommending his disciples to realize their capital and give it all away. No doubt he still calls some of his followers to do this today. But for most his command is to an inner detachment rather than to a literal renunciation. The New Testament does not imply that possessions are sinful in themselves.

Christ certainly meant us to put him above material wealth just as we are to put him above family ties. We cannot serve God and mammon. Moreover, we are to be conscientious in the use of our money. It is no longer ours. We hold it in stewardship from God. And in an era in which the gap between affluence and poverty is widening throughout the world, and in which the Christian missionary enterprise is severely hampered by lack of funds, we should be generous and disciplined in what we give away.

Time is every man's problem these days; and the newly converted Christian will undoubtedly have to rearrange his priorities. While he is a student, academic work will come high on the list. Christians should be known for their hard work and honesty. But he will also make time for new employments. He will have to carve out of his busy schedule time for daily prayer and Bible reading, for setting Sunday apart as the Lord's day which was instituted as a day of worship and rest, for fellowship with other Christians, for reading Christian literature, and for some kind of service in the church and the community.

All this is involved if we are to forsake sin and self, and follow Christ.

The call to confess Christ

We are commanded not only to follow Christ privately, but to confess him publicly. It is not enough to deny ourselves in secret if we deny him in the open. He said:

'Whoever is ashamed of me and of my words in this adulterous and sinful generation, of him will the Son of man also be ashamed, when he comes in the glory of his Father with the holy angels.'

'Every one who acknowledges me before men, I also will acknowledge before my Father who is in heaven; but whoever denies me before men, I also will deny before my Father who is in heaven.'[6]

Now the very fact that Jesus told us not to be ashamed of him shows that he knew we would be tempted to be ashamed; and the fact that he added 'in this adulterous and sinful generation' shows that he knew why. He evidently foresaw that his church would be a minority movement in the world; and it requires courage to side with the few against the many, especially if the few are unpopular and you may not be naturally drawn to them.

Yet this open confession of Christ cannot be avoided. Paul declared it to be a condition of salvation. In order to be saved, he wrote, we have not only to believe in our hearts but to confess with our lips that Jesus is Lord, 'for man believes with his heart and so is justified, and he confesses with his lips and so is saved'. The apostle may have been referring to baptism. Certainly, if not already baptized, the convert must be baptized, partly to receive through the application of water a visible sign and seal of his inward cleansing and new life in Christ, and partly to acknowledge publicly that he has trusted in Jesus Christ as his Saviour and Lord.

But the Christian's open confession does not end with his baptism. He must be willing for his family and friends to know he is a Christian, especially at first by the life he leads. This is bound in due course to lead to an opportunity for spoken witness, although he should be humble and honest here and not blunder tactlessly into other people's privacy. At the same time, he will join a church; associate himself with other

[6] Mark 8:38; Matthew 10:32, 33.

Christians at his college or place of business; not be afraid to own up to his Christian commitment when challenged about it; and start seeking by prayer, example and testimony to win his friends for Christ.

Incentives

The demands Jesus makes are heavy; but the reasons he gives are compelling. Indeed, if we are seriously to consider the total surrender for which he asks, we shall need these powerful incentives.

The first incentive is *for our own sake*.

'Whoever would save his life will lose it; and whoever loses his life . . . will save it. For what does it profit a man, to gain the whole world and forfeit his life? For what can a man give in return for his life?'[7]

Many people have a deep-seated fear that if they commit themselves to Jesus Christ, they will be the losers. They forget that Jesus came into the world that we might 'have life, and have it abundantly', that his purpose is to enrich not to impoverish, and that his service is perfect freedom.

Of course there are losses to face when we submit to Christ. We have already thought of the sin and self-centredness which we have to forsake; and we may lose some of our friends. But the rich and satisfying compensations far outweigh every loss. The astonishing paradox of Christ's teaching and of Christian experience is this: if we lose ourselves in following Christ, we actually find ourselves. True self-denial is true self-discovery. To live for ourselves is insanity and suicide; to live for God and for man is wisdom and life indeed. We do not begin to find ourselves until we have become willing to lose ourselves in the service of Christ and of our fellows.

To enforce this truth, Jesus placed in contrast the whole world and the individual soul. He then asked a businessman's question of profit and loss. Supposing you were to gain the whole world and lose yourself, he asked, what profit would you have made? He was arguing on the lowest level of personal

[7] Mark 8:35-37.

self-advantage, that to follow him is undoubtedly to have the best of the bargain. For to follow him is to find ourselves, whereas to hold on to ourselves and refuse to follow him is to lose ourselves and forfeit our eternal destiny, whatever material gains we may have made meanwhile. Why is this? Well, for one thing we cannot gain the whole world. For another, if we did, it would not last. And thirdly, while it did last, it would not satisfy. 'What can a man give in exchange for himself?' Nothing is valuable enough even to make an offer. Of course it costs to be a Christian; but it costs more not to be. It means losing oneself.

The second incentive for Christian commitment is *for the sake of others*. We should not submit to Christ only for what we get, but for what we can give. 'Whoever loses his life for . . . the gospel's sake, will save it.' 'For the sake of the gospel' means 'for the sake of proclaiming it to others'. We have already heard that we must not be ashamed of Christ or of his words; now we are to be so proud of him that we want to spread his good news to others.

Most of us feel oppressed by the heart-rending tragedy of this chaotic world. Our very survival is questionable. The ordinary citizen often feels a helpless victim of the tangled web of politics, or a faceless unit in the machine of modern society. But the Christian need not succumb to this sense of powerlessness. For Jesus Christ described his followers as both 'the salt of the earth' and 'the light of the world'. The use of salt before refrigeration had been invented was largely negative – to prevent decay in fish or meat. So Christians should stop society from deteriorating, by helping to preserve moral standards, influence public opinion and secure just legislation. As the light of the world Christians are to let their light shine. They have found in Jesus Christ the secret of peace and love, of personal relationships, of changing people; they must share their secret with others. The best contribution anyone can make to the supply of the world's need is to live a Christian life, build a Christian home, and radiate the light of the gospel of Jesus Christ.

The greatest incentive of all, however, is *for Christ's sake.* 'Whoever loses his life for my sake . . . will save it.' When we are asked to do something particularly hard, whether or not we are willing to do it depends very much on who asks us. If the request comes from someone who has a claim on us, and to whom we are indebted, we are glad to agree. This is why Christ's appeal to us is so eloquent and so persuasive. He asks us to deny ourselves and follow him for his own sake.

Surely this is why he describes the renunciation he demands as 'taking up the cross'. He asks no more than he gave. He asks a cross for a cross. We should follow him neither just for what we can get nor for what we can give, but supremely because of what he gave. He gave himself. Will it cost us much? It cost him more. He left the Father's glory, the immunities of heaven and the worship of countless angels when he came. He humbled himself to assume man's nature, to be born in a stable and laid in a manger, to work at a carpenter's bench, to make friends with rustic fisherfolk, to die on a common cross, and to bear the sins of the world.

Only a sight of the cross will make us willing to deny ourselves and follow Christ. Our little crosses are eclipsed by his. If we once catch a glimpse of the greatness of his love to suffer such shame and pain for us who deserved nothing but judgment, only one course of action will seem to be left. How can we deny or reject such a lover?

If, then, you suffer from moral anaemia, take my advice and steer clear of Christianity. If you want to live a life of easy-going self-indulgence, whatever you do, do not become a Christian. But if you want a life of self-discovery, deeply satisfying to the nature God has given you; if you want a life of adventure in which you have the privilege of serving him and your fellow men; if you want a life in which to express something of the overwhelming gratitude you are beginning to feel for him who died for you, then I would urge you to yield your life, without reserve and without delay, to your Lord and Saviour, Jesus Christ.

Your call is clear, cold centuries across;
You bid me follow you, and take my cross,
And daily lose myself, myself deny,
And stern against myself shout 'Crucify'.

My stubborn nature rises to rebel
Against your call. Proud choruses of hell
Unite to magnify my restless hate
Of servitude, lest I capitulate.

The world, to see my cross, would pause and jeer.
I have no choice, but still to persevere
To save myself – and follow you from far,
More slow than Magi – for I have no star.

And yet you call me still. Your cross
Eclipses mine, transforms the bitter loss
I thought that I would suffer if I came
To you – into immeasurable gain.

I kneel before you, Jesus, crucified,
My cross is shouldered and my self denied;
I'll follow daily, closely, not refuse
For love of you and man myself to lose.

10 REACHING A DECISION

That a decision is necessary in order to become a Christian is an idea quite foreign to many people. Some imagine that they are already Christians because they were born in a Christian country. 'After all,' they say, 'we are neither Jews, nor Mohammedans, nor Buddhists; so presumably we are Christians!' Others suppose that, having had a Christian upbringing, and having been taught to accept the Christian creed and Christian standards of behaviour, nothing further is required of them. But whatever his parentage and upbringing, every responsible adult is obliged to make up his own mind for or against Christ. We cannot remain neutral. Nor can we drift into Christianity. Nor can anybody else settle the matter for us. We must decide for ourselves.

Even agreement with all that has so far been written in this book is not sufficient. We may concede that the evidence for the deity of Jesus is compelling, even conclusive, and that he was in fact the Son of God; we may believe that he came and died to be the Saviour of the world; we may also admit that we are sinners and need such a Saviour. But none of these things makes us Christians, nor do all of them together. To believe certain facts about the person and work of Christ is a necessary preliminary, but true faith will translate such mental belief into a decisive act of trust. Intellectual conviction must lead to personal commitment.

I used myself to think that because Jesus had died on the cross, by some kind of rather mechanical transaction the whole world had been put right with God. I remember how puzzled, even indignant, I was when it was first suggested to me that I needed to appreciate Christ and his salvation for myself. I thank God that later he opened my eyes to see that I must do more than acknowledge I needed *a* Saviour, more even than acknowledge that Jesus Christ was *the* Saviour I needed; it was necessary to accept him as *my* Saviour. Certainly the personal pronoun is prominent in the Bible:

'The Lord is *my* shepherd, I shall not want.'

'The Lord is *my* light and *my* salvation.'

'O God, thou art *my* God.'

'The surpassing worth of knowing Christ Jesus *my* Lord.'

One verse in the Bible, which has helped many seekers (including myself) to understand the step of faith we have to take, contains the words of Christ himself. He says: 'Behold, I stand at the door and knock; if any one hears my voice and opens the door, I will come in to him and eat with him, and he with me.'[1]

This verse was illustrated by Holman Hunt in his well-known picture 'The Light of the World', painted in 1853. The original hangs in the chapel of Keble College, Oxford, and its replica (the artist's own work 40 years later) in St Paul's Cathedral. Although the pre-Raphaelites are out of fashion today, this picture's symbolism remains instructive. John Ruskin, in a letter to *The Times* in May 1854, described it in these words:

'. . . On the left-hand side of the picture is seen this door of the human soul. It is fast barred; its bars and nails are rusty; it is knitted and bound to its stanchions by creeping tendrils of ivy, showing that it has never been opened. A bat hovers about it; its threshold is over-grown with brambles, nettles and fruitless corn. . . . Christ approaches it in the night-time. . . . '

He is wearing a royal robe and a crown of thorns, holding a lantern in his left hand (as the light of the world) and knocking on the door with his right.

The context of the verse is illuminating. It comes at the end

[1] Revelation 3:20.

of a letter addressed by Christ through John to the church of Laodicea, situated in what is now Turkey. Laodicea was a prosperous city, renowned for its manufacture of clothing, its medical school where the famous Phrygian eye powder was made, and its wealthy banks.

Material prosperity had brought in its wake a spirit of complacency which had even contaminated the Christian church. Attached to it were professing Christians who proved to be Christian in name only. They were tolerably respectable, but nothing more. Their religious interest was shallow and casual. Like the water from the hot springs of Hierapolis which was piped to Laodicea by conduits (the remains of which can still be seen), they were (Jesus said) neither cold nor hot, but lukewarm, and therefore distasteful to him. Their spiritual tepidity is explained in terms of self-delusion: 'You say, "I am rich, I have prospered, and I need nothing"; not knowing that you are wretched, pitiable, poor, blind, and naked.'

What a description of proud and prosperous Laodicea! They were blind and naked beggars – naked despite their clothing factory, blind despite their Phrygian eye-salve, and beggars despite their banks.

We today are no different. Perhaps we say, as they did, 'I need nothing.' It would be hard to find any words more spiritually dangerous. It is our self-contained independence which, more than anything else, keeps us from committing ourselves to Christ. Of course we need him! Without him we are morally naked (with no clothing to fit us for God's presence), blind to spiritual truth, and beggars, having nothing with which to buy God's favour. But Christ can clothe us with his righteousness, touch our eyes into sight and enrich us with spiritual wealth. Apart from him, and until we open the door to admit him, we are blind and naked beggars.

'Behold, I stand at the door and knock', he says. He is no figment of the imagination, no fictitious character from a religious novel. This is the man of Nazareth, whose claims, character and resurrection warrant the conclusion that he is the Son of God. He is also the crucified Saviour. The hand that knocks is scarred. The feet which stand on the threshold still bear the print of nails.

And he is the risen Christ. John has already described him in the first chapter of Revelation, as he saw him in a highly symbolic vision. His eyes were like flaming fire and his feet like burnished brass. His voice thundered like the breakers on the rocks and his face was radiant like the sun shining in full strength. No wonder John fell at his feet. It is hard to understand how a person of such majesty could ever deign to visit poor, blind and naked beggars like ourselves.

Yet Jesus Christ says he is standing knocking at the door of our lives, waiting. Notice that he is standing at the door, not pushing it; speaking to us, not shouting. This is the more remarkable when we reflect that the house is his in any case. He is the architect; he designed it. He is the builder; he made it. He is the landlord; he bought it with his life-blood. So it is his by right of plan, construction and purchase. We are only tenants in a house which does not belong to us. He could put his shoulder to the door; he prefers to put his hand to the knocker. He could command us to open to him; instead, he merely invites us to do so. He will not force an entry into anybody's life. He says (verse 18) 'I counsel you . . .'. He could issue orders; he is content to give advice. Such are his condescension and humility, and the freedom he has given us.

But why does Jesus Christ want to come in? We know the answer already. He wants to be both our Saviour and our Lord.

He died to be our Saviour. If we receive him, he will be able to apply to us personally all the benefits of his death. Once inside the house, he will renovate, redecorate and refurnish it. That is, he will cleanse and forgive us; our past will be blotted out. He promises too to eat with us and allow us to eat with him. The phrase describes the joy of his companionship. He not only gives himself to us but asks us to give ourselves to him. We have been strangers; now we are friends. There has been a closed door between us; now we are seated at the same table.

Jesus Christ will also enter as our Lord and Master. The

house of our lives will come under his management, and there is no sense in opening the door unless we are willing for this. As he steps across the threshold, we must hand him our whole bunch of keys, granting him free access into every room. A fourth year Canadian student once wrote to me: 'Instead of giving Christ a whole set of different keys to the many rooms of the house ... I have given him a pass key to the whole lot.'

This involves repentance, turning resolutely from everything we know to be displeasing to him. Not that we make ourselves better before we invite him in. On the contrary, it is because we cannot forgive or improve ourselves that we need him to come to us. But we must be willing for him to do whatever rearranging he likes when he has come in. There can be no resistance, and no attempt to negotiate our own terms, but rather an unconditional surrender to the lordship of Christ. What will this mean? In detail I cannot tell you. In principle, it means a determination to forsake evil and follow Christ.

Do you hesitate? Do you say it is unreasonable to submit to Christ in the dark? Surely it is not. It is much more reasonable than marriage. In marriage a man and a woman commit themselves to each other without condition. They do not know what the future holds for them. But they love each other, and they trust each other. So they promise to take each other, 'to have and to hold from this day forward, for better for worse, for richer for poorer, in sickness and in health, to love and to cherish, till death us do part'. If humans can thus trust humans, can we not trust God's Son? It is more reasonable to commit oneself to the divine Christ than to the finest and noblest of human beings. He will never betray or abuse our confidence.

So what must we do? To begin with, we must hear his voice. It is tragically possible to turn a deaf ear to Christ and drown the insistent whisper of his appeal. Sometimes we hear his voice through the prickings of the conscience, sometimes through the gropings of the mind. Or it may be a moral defeat, or the seeming emptiness and meaninglessness of our existence, or an inexplicable spiritual hunger, or sickness, bereavement, pain or fear, by which we become aware that Christ is outside the door and speaking to us. Or his call can come to us through a friend, a preacher or a book. Whenever we hear, we must listen. 'He who has ears to hear,' Jesus says, 'let him hear.'

Next, we must open the door. Having heard his voice, we must open to his knock. To open the door to Jesus Christ is a pictorial way of describing an act of faith in him as our Saviour, an act of submission to him as our Lord.

It is a definite act. The tense of the Greek verb makes this plain. The door does not happen to swing open by chance. Nor is it already ajar. It is closed, and needs to be opened. Moreover, Christ will not open the door himself. There is neither handle nor latch on the door in Holman Hunt's picture. It is said that he omitted them deliberately, to show that the handle was on the inside. Christ knocks; but we must open.

It is an individual act. True, the message was sent to a church, the nominal, lukewarm church of Laodicea. But the challenge is addressed to individuals within it: 'If *anyone* hears my voice and opens the door, I will come in to him.' Every man must make his own decision and take this step himself. Nobody else can do it for you. Christian parents and teachers, ministers and friends can point the way, but your hand and only yours can draw back the bolts and turn the handle.

It is a unique act. You can take this step only once. When Christ has entered, he will bolt and bar the door on the inside. Sin may drive him into the cellar or the attic, but he will never altogether abandon the house he has entered. 'I will never fail you nor forsake you,' he says. This is not to say that you emerge from this experience with the fully grown wings of an angel! Nor that you will become perfect in the twinkling of an eye. You can become a Christian in a moment, but not a mature Christian. Christ can enter, cleanse and forgive you in a matter of seconds, but it will take much longer for your character to be transformed and moulded to his will. It takes only a few minutes for a bride and bridegroom to be married, but in the rough-and-tumble of their home it may take many years for two strong wills to be dovetailed into one. So when we receive Christ, a moment of commitment will lead to a lifetime of adjustment.

It is a deliberate act. You do not have to wait for a supernatural light to flash upon you from heaven, or for an emotional experience to overtake you. No. Christ came into the world and died for your sins. He has now come and stood outside the front door of the house of your life, and he is knocking. The next move is yours. His hand is already on the knocker; your hand must now feel for the latch.

It is an urgent act. Do not wait longer than you must. Time is passing. The future is uncertain. You may never have a better opportunity than this. 'Do not boast about tomorrow, for you do not know what a day may bring forth.' 'The Holy Spirit says, "Today, when you hear his voice, do not harden your hearts . . .".'[2] Do not put it off until you have tried to make yourself better or worthier of Christ's entry; or until you have solved all your problems. If you believe that Jesus Christ is the Son of God and that he died to be your Saviour, that is enough. The rest will follow in due time. True, there is danger in rash and precipitate action; but there is equal danger in procrastination. If in your heart of hearts you know that you should act, then you should not delay any longer.

It is an indispensable act. Of course there is much more to the Christian life than this. As we shall see in the next chapter, there is getting into the fellowship of the church, discovering and doing God's will, growing in grace and understanding, and seeking to serve God and man; but this step is the beginning, and nothing else will do instead. You can believe in Christ intellectually and admire him; you can say your prayers to him through the keyhole (I did for many years); you can push coins at him under the door to keep him quiet; you can be moral, decent, upright and good; you can be religious; you can have been baptized and confirmed; you can be deeply versed in the philosophy of religion; you can be a theological student and even an ordained minister – and still not have opened the door to Christ. There is no substitute for this.

[2] Proverbs 27:1; Hebrews 3:7, 8.

A university professor describes in his autobiography how he was travelling one day on the top of a bus when

> 'without words and (I think) almost without images, a fact about myself was somehow presented to me. I became aware that I was holding something at bay, or shutting something out. Or, if you like, that I was wearing some stiff clothing, like corsets, or even a suit of armour, as if I were a lobster. I felt myself being, there and then, given a free choice. I could open the door or keep it shut; I could unbuckle the armour or keep it on. Neither choice was presented as a duty; no threat or promise was attached to either, though I knew that to open the door or to take off the corset meant the incalculable . . . I chose to open, to unbuckle, to loosen the rein. I say "I chose", yet it did not really seem possible to do the opposite.'

So Professor C. S. Lewis describes his experience in *Surprised by Joy*.

A titled lady responded to Billy Graham's invitation to go forward at the end of an evangelistic meeting. She was introduced to an adviser who, discovering that she had not yet committed her life to Christ, suggested that she should pray there and then. Bowing her head, she said, 'Dear Lord Jesus, I want you to come into my heart more than anything else in the world. Amen.'

A boy in his later teens knelt at his bedside one Sunday night in the dormitory of his school. In a simple, matter-of-fact but definite way he told Christ that he had made rather a mess of life so far; he confessed his sins; he thanked Christ for dying for him; and he asked him to come into his life. The following day he wrote in his diary:

> 'Yesterday really *was* an eventful day! . . . Up till now Christ has been on the circumference and I have but asked him to guide me instead of giving him complete control. Behold, he stand at the door and knocks. I have heard him and now he has come into my house. He has cleansed it and now rules in it. . . . '

And the day after:

> 'I really have felt an immense and new joy throughout today. It is the joy of being at peace with the world and of being in touch with God. How well do I know now that he rules me and that I never really knew him before. . . . '

These are extracts from my own diary. I venture to quote them because I do not want you to think that I am recommending to you a step which I have not taken myself.

Are you a Christian? A real and committed Christian? Your answer depends on another question – not whether you go to church or not, believe the creed or not, or lead a decent life or not (important as all these are in their place), but rather this: which side of the door is Jesus Christ? Is he inside or outside? That is the crucial issue.

Perhaps you are ready to open the door to Christ. If you are not sure whether you have ever done so, my advice to you would be to make sure, even if (as someone has put it) you will be going over in ink what you have already written in pencil.

I suggest that you get away and alone to pray. Confess your sins to God, and forsake them. Thank Jesus Christ that he died for your sake and in your place. Then open the door and ask him to come in as your personal Saviour and Lord.

You might find it a help to echo this prayer in your heart:

'Lord Jesus Christ, I acknowledge that I have gone my own way. I have sinned in thought, word and deed. I am sorry for my sins. I turn from them in repentance.

I believe that you died for me, bearing my sins in your own body. I thank you for your great love.

Now I open the door. Come in, Lord Jesus. Come in as my Saviour, and cleanse me. Come in as my Lord, and take control of me. And I will serve as you give me strength, all my life. Amen.'

If you have prayed this prayer and meant it, humbly thank Christ that he has come in. For he said he would. He has given his word: 'If any one hears my voice and opens the door, *I will come in* to him. . . .' Disregard your feelings; trust his promise; and thank him that he has kept his word.

11 BEING A CHRISTIAN

This last chapter is written for those who have opened the door of their lives to Jesus Christ. They have committed themselves to him. They have thus begun the Christian life. But *becoming* a Christian is one thing; *being* a Christian is another. It is with the implications of being a Christian that we must now concern ourselves.

You took a simple step; you invited Christ to come as your Saviour and Lord. At that moment what can only be described as a miracle took place. God – without whose grace you could not have repented and believed – gave you a new life. You were born again. You became a child of God and so entered his family. You may not have been conscious of anything happening, even as at the time of your physical birth you were not conscious of what was taking place. Self-consciousness, the awareness of who and what one is, is part of the process of personal development. Nevertheless, just as when you were born you emerged as a new independent personality, so when you were born again you became spiritually a new creature in Christ.

But (you may be thinking) is not God the Father of all men? Are not all people the children of God? Yes and no! God is certainly the creator of all men, and all are his 'offspring' in the sense that they derive their being from him.[1] But the Bible clearly distinguishes between this general relation of God to the whole human race as Creator to creature and the special relation of father to child which he establishes with those who

[1] See, for example, Acts 17:28.

130

are his new creation through Jesus Christ. John explains this in the prologue to his Gospel when he writes:

'He (that is, Jesus) came to his own home, and his own people received him not. But to all who received him, who believed in his name, he gave power to become children of God; who were born ... of God.'

The three clauses beginning with the word 'who' all describe the same people. The children of God are those who are born of God; and those who are born of God are those who have received Christ into their lives and who have believed in his name.

What does it mean to be a 'child' of God in this sense? Like membership of any other family, it has both its privileges and its responsibilities. We must now go on to see what these are.

Christian privileges

The unique privilege of the person who has been born anew into the family of God is that he is related to God. Let us consider this relationship.

An intimate relationship

We saw earlier that our sins had alienated us from God. They had come as a barrier between us. Put differently, we were under the just condemnation of the Judge of all the earth. But now through Jesus Christ, who bore our condemnation and to whom by faith we have become united, we have been 'justified', that is, brought into acceptance with God and pronounced righteous. Our Judge has become our Father.

'See what love the Father has given us, that we should be called children of God; and so we are', wrote John. 'Father' and 'Son' are the distinctive titles which Jesus gave to God and to himself, and they are the very names which he permits us to use! By union with him we are permitted to share something of his own intimate relation to the Father. Cyprian, Bishop of Carthage in the middle of the third century AD, well expresses our privilege when writing about the Lord's Prayer:

> 'How great is the Lord's indulgence! How great are his condescension and plenteousness of goodness towards us, seeing that he has wished us to pray in the sight of God in such a way as to call God Father, and to call ourselves sons of God, even as Christ is the Son of God – a name which none of us would dare to venture on in prayer, unless he himself had allowed us thus to pray.'

Now at last we can repeat the Lord's Prayer without hypocrisy. Previously the words had a hollow sound; now they ring with new and noble meaning. God is indeed our Father in heaven, who knows our needs before we ask and will not fail to give good things to his children.

It may be necessary for us sometimes to receive correction at his hand, 'for the Lord disciplines him whom he loves, and chastises every son whom he receives.' But in this he is treating us as sons and disciplining us for our good. With such a Father, loving, wise and strong, we can be delivered from all our fears.[2]

An assured relationship

The Christian's relationship to God as a child to his Father is not only intimate, but sure. So many people seem to do no more than hope for the best; it is possible to know for certain.

It is more than possible. It is God's revealed will for us. We ought to be sure of our relationship with God not just for the sake of our peace of mind and helpfulness to others, but because God means us to be sure. John states categorically that this was his purpose in writing his first letter; 'I write this to you who believe in the name of the Son of God, that you may know that you have eternal life.'

Yet the way to *be* sure is not just to *feel* sure. Most people who are at the beginning of their Christian life make this mistake. They rely too much on their superficial feelings. One day they *feel* close to God; the next day they *feel* estranged from him again. And since they imagine that their feelings accurately reflect their spiritual condition, they fall into a frenzy of uncertainty. Their Christian life becomes a precarious switch-

[2] For our heavenly Father's care see Matthew 6:7-13, 25-34 and 7:7-12, and for his discipline Hebrews 12:3-11.

back ride as they soar to the heights of elation, only to plunge again into the depths of depression.

This erratic experience is not God's purpose for his children. We have to learn to mistrust our feelings. They are extremely variable. They change with the weather, with circumstances and with our health. We are fickle creatures of whim and mood, and our fluctuating feelings often have nothing to do with our spiritual progress.

The basis of our knowledge that we are in relationship with God is not our feelings, but the fact that he says we are. The test we are to apply to ourselves is objective rather than subjective. We are not to grub around inside ourselves for evidence of spiritual life, but to look up and out and away to God and his word. But where shall we find God's word to assure us that we are his children?

First, God promises in his written word to give eternal life to those who receive Christ. 'This is the testimony, that God gave us eternal life, and this life is in his Son. He who has the Son has life; he who has not the Son has not life.' Humbly to believe that we have eternal life is not then presumptuous. On the contrary, to believe God's word is humility not pride, and wisdom not presumption. The folly and the sin would be to doubt, for 'he who does not believe God, has made him a liar, because he has not believed in the testimony that God has borne to his son'.[3]

Now the Bible is full of the promises of God. The sensible Christian begins as soon as possible to store them in his memory. Then when he falls into the ditch of depression and doubt, he can use God's promises as ropes by which to pull himself out.

Here are a few verses to start memorizing. Each contains a divine promise.[4]

Christ will receive us if we come to him: John 6:37.

He will hold us and never let us go: John 10:28.

[3] 1 John 5:10-12.

[4] See also *Some Basic Texts* (Inter-Varsity Press), a classified selection of 150 passages for memorizing.

He will never leave us: Matthew 28:20; Hebrews 13:5, 6.

God will not allow us to be tempted beyond our strength: 1 Corinthians 10:13.

He will forgive us when we confess our sins: 1 John 1:9.

He will give us wisdom when we ask for it: James 1:5.

Second, God speaks to our hearts. Listen to these statements. 'God's love has been poured into our hearts through the Holy Spirit . . .' and 'When we cry, "Abba! Father!" it is the Spirit himself bearing witness with our spirit that we are the children of God.'[5] Every Christian knows what this means. The outward witness of the Holy Spirit in Scripture is confirmed by the inward witness of the Holy Spirit in experience. This is not to place any confidence in shallow and changeable feelings; it is rather to expect a deepening conviction in our hearts as the Holy Spirit assures us of God's love for us and prompts us to cry 'Father!' as we seek God's face in prayer.

Third, the same Spirit who bears witness to our sonship in Scripture and experience completes his testimony in our character. If we are born again into God's family, then God's Spirit dwells within us. Indeed, the indwelling of the Holy Spirit is one of the greatest privileges of God's children. It is their distinguishing characteristic: 'For all who are led by the Spirit of God are sons of God.' Again, 'Anyone who does not have the Spirit of Christ does not belong to him.'[6] And he will not have indwelt us long before he begins to work a change in our manner of life. John applies this test ruthlessly in his first letter. If anyone persists in disobeying the commandments of God and in disregarding his duties to his fellow men, he writes, then he is not a Christian, whatever he may say. Righteousness and love are indispensable marks of the child of God.

A secure relationship

Supposing we have entered into this intimate relationship with God, and are assured of it by God's own word, is it a secure

5 Romans 5:5; 8:15,16.
6 See Romans 8:9-17.

relationship? Or can we be born into God's family one moment and repudiated from it the next? The Bible indicates that it is a permanent relationship. 'If children, then heirs,' wrote Paul, 'heirs of God and fellow heirs with Christ', and went on to argue, in a magnificent passage at the end of Romans 8, that God's children are eternally safe, for nothing whatever can separate them from his love.

'But what happens if and when I sin?' you may ask. 'Do I then forfeit my sonship and cease to be God's child?' No. Think of the analogy of a human family. A boy is offensively rude to his parents. A cloud descends on the home. There is tension in the atmosphere. Father and son are not on speaking terms. What has happened? Has the boy ceased to be a son? No. Their relationship has not changed; it is their fellowship which has been broken. Relationship depends on birth; fellowship depends on behaviour. As soon as the boy apologizes, he is forgiven. And forgiveness restores fellowship. Meanwhile, his relationship has remained the same. He may have been temporarily a disobedient, and even a defiant, son; but he has not ceased to be a son.

So it is with the children of God. When we sin, we do not forfeit our relationship to him as children, though our fellowship with him is spoiled until we confess and forsake our sin. As soon as we 'confess our sins, he is faithful and just, and will forgive our sins and cleanse us from all unrighteousness', for 'if any one does sin, we have an advocate with the Father, Jesus Christ the righteous; and he is the expiation for our sins'.[7] So do not wait until the evening, still less the following Sunday, to put right whatever has gone wrong during each day. Instead, when you fall, fall on your knees and repent and humbly seek your Father's forgiveness at once. Aim to preserve your conscience clear and undefiled.

Put in another way, we can be justified only once; but we need to be forgiven every day. When Jesus washed the apostles' feet, he gave them an illustration of this. Peter asked him to wash his hands and his head as well as his feet. But Jesus

[7] 1 John 1:9; 2:1, 2.

replied: 'He who has bathed does not need to wash, except for his feet, but he is clean all over.' A man invited to a dinner party in Jerusalem would take a bath before going out. On arrival at his friend's house, he would not be offered another bath; but a slave would meet him at the front door and wash his feet. So when we first come to Christ in repentance and faith, we receive a 'bath' (which is justification, and is outwardly symbolized in baptism). It never needs to be repeated. But as we walk through the dusty streets of the world, we constantly need to 'have our feet washed' (which is daily forgiveness).

Christian responsibilities

To be a child of God is a wonderful privilege. It involves obligations also. Peter implied this when he wrote: 'Like newborn babes, long for the pure spiritual milk, that by it you may grow up to salvation.'[8]

The great privilege of the child of God is relationship; his great responsibility is growth. Everybody loves children, but nobody in his right mind wants them stay in the nursery. The tragedy, however, is that many Christians, born again in Christ, never grow up. Others even suffer from spiritual infantile regression. Our heavenly Father's purpose, on the other hand, is that 'babes in Christ' should become 'mature in Christ'. Our birth must be followed by growth. The crisis of justification (our acceptance before God) must lead to the process of sanctification (our growth in holiness, what Peter terms 'growing up to salvation').

There are two main spheres in which the Christian is meant to grow. The first is in understanding and the second in holiness. When we begin the Christian life, we probably understand very little, and we have only just come to know God. Now we must increase in the knowledge of God and of our Lord and Saviour, Jesus Christ. This knowledge is partly intellectual and partly personal. In connection with

[8] 1 Peter 2:2.

the former, I would urge you not only to study the Bible but to read good Christian books. To neglect to grow in your understanding is to court disaster.

We must also grow in holiness of life. The New Testament writers speak of the development of our faith in God, our love for our fellow men and our likeness to Christ. Every son of God longs to become more and more conformed in his character and behaviour to the Son of God himself. The Christian life is a life of righteousness. We must seek to obey God's commandments and do God's will. The Holy Spirit has been given us partly for this purpose. He has made our bodies his temple. He dwells within us. And as we submit to his authority and follow his leading, he will subdue our evil desires and cause his fruit to appear in our lives, which is 'love, joy, peace, patience, kindness, goodness, faithfulness, gentleness, self-control'.[9]

But how shall we grow? There are three main secrets of spiritual development. They are also the chief responsibilities of the child of God.

Our duty to God
Our relationship to our heavenly Father, though secure, is not static. He wants his children to grow up to know him more and more intimately. Generations of Christians have discovered that the principal way to do so is to wait upon him every day in a time of Bible reading and prayer. This is an indispensable necessity for the Christian who wants to make progress. We are all busy nowadays, but we must somehow rearrange our priorities in order to make time for it. It will mean rigorous self-discipline, but granted this, together with a legible Bible and an alarm clock that works, we are well on the road to victory.

It is important to preserve the balance between Bible reading and prayer, because through Scripture God speaks to us while through prayer we speak to him. It is also wise to be systematic in our reading of the Bible. Various methods are

[9] Galatians 5:16, 22, 23.

available.[10] Pray before you read, asking the Holy Spirit to open your eyes and illumine your mind. Then read slowly, meditatively and thoughtfully. Read and re-read the passage. Wrestle with it till it yields its meaning. Use a modern translation. The Revised Standard Version is probably the most accurate revision available in contemporary English. You may also find a good commentary a help.[11] Then go on to apply to your own circumstances the message of the verses you have read. Look for promises to claim and commands to obey, examples to follow and sins to avoid. It is helpful to keep a notebook and write down what you learn. Above all, look for Jesus Christ. He is the chief subject of the Bible. We can not only find him revealed there, but can meet him personally through its pages.

Prayer follows naturally. Begin by speaking back to God on the same subject on which he has spoken to you. Don't change the conversation! If he has spoken to you of himself and his glory, worship him. If he has spoken to you of yourself and your sins, confess them. Thank him for any blessings which may have been revealed in the passage, and pray that its lessons may be learned by yourself and your friends.

When you have prayed over the Bible passage you have read, you will want to go on with other prayers. If your Bible is the first great aid to prayer, your diary will be the second. Commit to him in the morning the details of the day which lies before you, and in the evening run through the day again, confessing the sins you have committed, giving thanks for the blessings you have received and praying for the people you have met.

God is your Father. Be natural, confiding and bold. He

[10] Scripture Union publish schemes and notes for various age-groups and interests. Inter-Varsity Press publish for students and others *Hold the Faith* (an introductory course) and *Search the Scriptures* (a three-year course). The IVP booklet *The Quiet Time* has some very valuable advice about daily prayer and Bible reading.

[11] For instance, *The New Bible Commentary,* revised edition edited by D. Guthrie, J. A. Motyer, A. M. Stibbs and D. J. Wiseman (Inter-Varsity Press, 1970).

is interested in all the details of your life. Very soon you will find it essential to start some kind of prayer list of your relatives and friends for whom you feel a responsibility to pray. It is wise to make your list as flexible as possible, so that people can be easily added to it or taken from it.

Our duty to the church

The Christian life is not just a private affair of your own. If we are born again into God's family, not only has he become our Father but every other believer in the world, whatever his nation or denomination, has become our brother or sister in Christ. One of the commonest names for Christians in the New Testament is 'brethren'. This is a glorious truth. But it is no good supposing that membership of the universal church of Christ is enough; we must belong to some local branch of it. Nor is it sufficient to be a member of a Christian Union in a college or elsewhere (although I hope you will become active in yours). Every Christian's place is in a local church, sharing in its worship, fellowship and witness.

Perhaps you ask which church you should join. If you are already linked with a church, either by upbringing or because you have been attending one recently, you would be unwise to sever this connection without good reason. If you are free to choose your church membership, however, here are two criteria to guide you. The first concerns the minister, the second the congregation. Ask yourself these questions. Is the minister submissive to the authority of Scripture, so that he seeks in his sermons to explain its message and relate it to contemporary life? And does the congregation at least approximate to a fellowship of believers who love Christ, one another and the world?

Baptism is the way of entry into the visible Christian society. It has other meanings as well, as we have seen, but if you have not been baptized, you should ask your minister to prepare you for baptism. Then do allow yourself to be drawn right into the Christian fellowship. Much may seem strange to you at first, but do not stand aside. Church or chapel attendance on Sundays is a definite Christian duty, and nearly every branch of the Christian church agrees that the Lord's Supper or Holy Communion is the central service, instituted by Christ and commemorating his death in fellowship with one another.

I hope I am not giving the impression that fellowship is merely a Sunday treat! Love for other Christians, however unlikely it may seem in prospect, is a new and real experience. In a Christian fellowship of all types, backgrounds and ages, there are new depths of friendship and mutual sharing to be discovered. The Christian's closest friends will probably be Christians and, above all, his life partner must be a Christian too. [12]

Our duty to the world

The Christian life is a family affair, in which the children enjoy fellowship with their Father and with each other. But let it not for one moment be thought that this exhausts the Christian's responsibilities. Christians are not a self-regarding coterie of smug and selfish prigs, who are interested only in themselves. On the contrary, every Christian should be deeply concerned about all his fellow men. And it is part of his Christian vocation to serve them in whatever way he can.

The Christian church has a noble record of philanthropic work for the needy and neglected people of the world – the poor and hungry, the sick, the victims of oppression and discrimination, slaves, prisoners, orphans, refugees and drop-outs. Still today all over the world the followers of Christ are seeking in his name to alleviate suffering and distress. Yet an enormous amount of work is waiting to be done. And sometimes, it must be confessed with shame, others who make no Christian profession seem to show more compassion than we who claim to know Christ.

There is another and particular responsibility which Christians have towards 'the world', as the Bible describes those outside Christ and his church: evangelism. To 'evangelize' means literally to spread the good news of Jesus Christ. There are still millions of people who are ignorant of him and

[12] See, for instance, 2 Corinthians 6:14.

his salvation, not only in Asia, Africa and Latin America, but in the secularized Western world as well. For centuries the church seems to have been half asleep. Is this the generation in which Christians will wake up and win the world for Christ? Perhaps he has a special task for you to do as an ordained minister of the gospel or as a missionary. If you are a student already launched on your course, it would be quite wrong for you to do anything rash or hasty. But seek to discover God's will for your life, and be surrendered to it.

Although every Christian is not called to be a minister or a missionary, God does intend every Christian to be a witness to Jesus Christ. In his own home, among his friends in his college or at his place of business, it is his solemn responsibility to live a consistent, loving, humble, honest, Christ-like life, and to seek to win other people for him. He will be discreet and courteous, but determined.

The way to begin is by prayer. Ask God to give you a special concern for one or two of your friends. It is usually wise to keep to people of your own sex and about your own age. Then pray regularly and definitely for their conversion; foster your friendship with them for its own sake; take trouble to spend time with them; and really love them for themselves. Soon an opportunity will come to take them to some service or meeting where they will hear the gospel explained; or to give them some Christian literature to read; or to tell them simply what Jesus Christ has come to mean to you and how you found him. I need hardly add that our most eloquent testimony will be without effect if we are contradicting it by our conduct; while little is more influential for Christ than a life which he is obviously transforming.

Such are the great privileges and responsibilities of the child of God. Born into the family of God and enjoying with his heavenly Father a relationship which is intimate, assured and secure, he seeks to be disciplined in his daily times of Bible reading and prayer, loyal in his church membership, and at the same time active in Christian service and witness.

This statement of the Christian life reveals the tension to which all Christian people are subject. In brief, we find ourselves citizens of two kingdoms, the one earthly and the other heavenly. And each citizenship lays upon us duties which we are not at liberty to evade.

On the one hand, the New Testament writers lay considerable stress on our obligations to the state, to our employer, to our family and to society as a whole. The Bible will not allow us to retreat from these practical responsibilities either into mysticism, or into a monastery, or even into a Christian fellowship which is insulated from the world.

On the other hand, some New Testament authors remind us that we are 'aliens and exiles' on earth, that 'our commonwealth is in heaven' and that we are travelling to an eternal home.[13] Consequently, we are not to lay up treasures on earth, nor to pursue purely selfish ambitions, nor to become assimilated to the standards of the world, nor to be unduly burdened by the sorrows of this present life.

It is comparatively simple to ease this tension either by withdrawing into Christ and neglecting the world, or by so involving ourselves in the world as to forget Christ. Neither of these is a genuinely Christian solution, however, since each involves the denial of one or other of our Christian obligations. The balanced Christian who takes Scripture for his guide will seek to live equally and simultaneously 'in Christ' and 'in the world'. He cannot opt out of either.

This is the life of discipleship to which Jesus Christ calls us. He died and rose again that we might have newness of life. He has given us his Spirit so that we can live out this life in the world.

Now he calls us to follow him, to give ourselves wholly and unreservedly to his service.

[13] See, for example, 1 Peter 2:11; Philippians 3:20; 2 Corinthians 4:16-18.

GREECE

The infinite variety of the landscape of mainland Greece, ranging from snowcapped rugged mountains to sundrenched idyllic beaches, is equalled, if not surpassed, by the beauty of the seascape of almost one thousand five hundred islands scattered over the translucent waters of the Aegean and Ionian Seas. Close to nine million inhabitants live on the 51.182 square miles, which are blessed by a temperate climate under the blue sky of the Mediterranean.

Five thousand years of dramatic history have left their indelible imprint, rivalling nature in its diversity, from the Minoan palaces, Mycenaean fortresses, classical temples, Hellenistic tombs, Roman towns, Byzantine churches, Crusader castles, Turkish mosques and the picturesque villages of the distinctive island architecture to the pleasing modernity of the main cities, spas and summer resorts.

Each region displays a characteristic brand of natural and artistic features which, nevertheless, only serve to emphasise the unity of Europe's oldest culture, the craddle of western civilisation. no wonder that a people looking back on such a glorious past has preserved in its purest and most welcome form the traditional hospitality towards all strangers visiting their lovely country.

Between 4.000 and 3.000 B.C. the Minoans settled in the southern island of Crete, with 3.327 square miles Greece's largest, and founded one of the most brilliant and sophisticated civilisations of antiquity, and Europe's first. Mythology and history blend in the Priest - King Minos, the legendary son of Zeus, ruler of the Olympian gods, and Europa, the lovely princess after whom the continent is named. From his splendid palace at Knossos, successive Minos ruled the world's first naval empire, which was destroyed by the eruption of the island volcano of Thira, a Cretan colony, in about 1450 B.C. According to some archaeologists this was the lost island of Atlantis, and the recent discovery of a whole town under 160 feet of lava and pumice lends credibility to this theory.

History then shifts to the mainland, where for a thousand years Hellenic tribes, Pelasgians, Achaeans, Aeolians and Ionians had infiltrated from the north, subdued the native Celts and established numerous small principalities following the country's natural division by impassable mountain ranges.

In the eighth century B.C. the great epic poet Homer was to immortalise the Mycenaean age in the *Iliad* and *Odyssey*, the story of the Trojan War fought by Achilles, Odysseus and countless other heroes under the leadership of the High King Agamemnon to bring back the beautiful Helen, wife of King Menelaus of Sparta. Long believed to be nothing but poetic fantasy, the German amateur archaeologist Heinrich Schliemann vindicated Homer's historical accuracy by following the poets geographical indications to the letter to unearth in the 1870s the palaces and towns of the epic cycle.

In about 1100B.C. the magnificent Bronze Age civilisation of the Mycenaeans fell to the iron weapons of a new invader from the north, the blond, blue-eyed Dorians. Warlike feudal kingdoms emerged from the Dark Ages at the dawn of recorded history in the ninth century B.C. and in the following six-hundred years the Greeks tried and often invented every political system the human mind has as yet conceived. As a tribute to their experimentations, most forms of government still bear the Greek name indicative of their origin.

Tribal, feudal, absolute and constitutional monarchy, landed and commercial oligarchy, Spartan racism followed by a short spell of communism, dictatorships of all kinds, democracy where the active participation of all citizens was possible due to slavery, decline into demagogy which made the anachronistic city states an easy prey to the unified Macedonian kingdom of Philip, who laid the foundations on which his son Alexander the Great could build his world empire.

The great names in this period are Lycurgus, who imposed a totalitarian way of life on Sparta in the eighth century B.C.; Dracon and Solon, the latter one of the Seven Wise of Antiquity, who brought law and order to Athens in the two subsequent centuries; Miltiades, who defeated the Persians at Marathon in 490 B.C. in one of the decisive battles in the eternal struggle between Europe and Asia; Themistocles, who brought this struggle to a victorious climax at the battle of Salamis 10 years later, by the use of seapower which assured Athens of mastery in the Aegean for the entire fifth century B.C. Yet like his predecessor Miltiades, who had died in prison, he fell a victim to the jealousy of his ungrateful Athenian compatriots, who not only ostracised him — exile for ten years without any accusation and thus no means of defence — but eventually condemned him to death, so that the saviour of Greece had to seek refuge at the court of the Persian king he had so brilliantly defeated; and Pausanias, the Spartan regent who finally drove the Persians from Greek soil in the battle of Plataea in 479 B.C., but succumbed to Persian bribes and was stoned to death, his mother reputedly throwing the first stone.

The billiant generalship of Kimon extended the Athenian empire along the shores of Asia Minor, so that when he in his turn was ostracised in 461 B.C., Pericles presided over the Golden Age of unparalleled intellectual and artistic achievements, coinciding with a political decline, almost imperceptible at first, but leading to the outbreak of the disastrous Peloponnesian War (431-404 B.C.) in which the personification of Greek virtues and vices, Alcibiades, played the leading part. The year of Athens' final defeat and humiliation also witnessed his murder.

Spartan dominance was challenged in the next century by the military genius of Epaminondas, who briefly established Theban supremacy by introducing a new fighting force, the phalanx, which was perfected by Philip of Macedonia and assured his victory over the for once united Greek city states at Chaeronea in 338 B.C. Philip generously forgave his main opponent, the Athenian orator Demosthenes, who yet succeeded in persuading the Greeks to another stand against the Macedonians after Philip's murder two years later.

The insurrection was swiftly crushed by young Alexander, who ruthlessly destroyed Thebes but spared Athens for its cultural prestige. He forced the reluctant Greek states to follow him in his expedition into Persia and in 334 B.C. he crossed the Hellespont at the head of a mere 40.000 men to the greatest conquest the world had ever seen. In eleven years of unbroken victories, Alexander founded an empire that stretched from the Ionian Sea to beyond the Indus, and from the Upper Nile to the Caspian Sea. But the center of gravity had shifted from Macedonia to Babylon, where Alexander died in 323 B.C., having failed in welding Greeks and Persians into a new imperial master race.

In the deadly struggle for the succession, Demetrius Poliorcetes (Besieger of Towns) lost Asia but gained the Greek-Macedonian kingdom, over which the Atnigonid dynasty ruled precariously till the Roman conquest in 146 B.C. Yet Greece achieved a remarkable cultural conquest-in-reverse, and the Roman empire became impregnated with the higher art and thought of Greece, to which the Roamn aristocracy sent its sons for education in the schools of Athens and Rhodes.

In exchange the Romans used Greece as the battleground for the momentous civil wars of the first century B.C. In 48 B.C. Pompey's numerically superior army was crushingly defeated by julius Caesar at Pharsala in Thessaly. In 42 B.C. Brutus kept his fatal appointment with Caesar's ghost at Philippi in Macedonia, where Brutus and Cassius committed suicide, while Mark Antony and Octavian divided the world in preparation for the final round. That came in 31 B.C. at the naval battle of Actium, where Cleopatra precipitated Antony into unreasonable flight and another double suicide, leaving Octavian sole ruler and at last able to establish the Pax Romana for some four hundred years.

The Roman emperors varied in the treatment of their most precious province from Nero, who shipped priceless statues by the hundred to Italy, to Hadrian, who munificently embellished the venerable centers of culture. Roman tourists flocked to the famous sites, so not quite in the same numbers as today.

In the partition of the Roman Empire in the fourth century A.D., Greece was alloted to the Eastern Empire. The new capital,

Constantinople, was adorned with the spoils from Greece, while pious Byzantine emperors closed the pagan universities and temples. Successive waves of barbaric tribes, Goths, Huns, Vandals and Avars ravaged the country with fire and sword, joined by Saracen pirates, bringing in their wake Slav settlers who threatened to engulf the mainland till Basill II the Bulgar-Slayer decisively stopped the flood.

After the conquest of Constantinople by the Fourth Crusade in 1204, feudalism returned to the country which had experienced an earlier version in Mycenaean times. Under the nominal suzerainty of the Latin emperor, the Frankish lords were fighting each other as much as the renascent Byzantines, Bulgarians, Serbs, Catalan mercenaries and soon the advance guard of the Turks. The dying Byzantine empire achieved a final but hollow triumph with the reconquest of the Peloponnese in 1430, where two brothers of the last emperor ruled for another six years after his death in the defence of his capital. But in 1460 they were driven out by Sultan Mohammed II, who replaced the Frankish and Byzantine nobles with Turkish veterans. The Greek peasants remained serfs, paying besides tithes a poll-tax and a blood tribute of a fifth of their male children, who were brought up as Moslems and enrolled in the corps of Janissaries, the military élite of the Turkish armies. The frequent incursions and temporary occupation by the Venetians only worsened the lot of the wretched inhabitants, whose only protector was their recognised representative, the Patriarch of Constantinople, while the bishops provided local guidance and the parochial clergy the little education there was.

In their decline the Turks became only interested in the collection of tribute, while the country was reduced to a state of anarchy, from which a military adventurer, Ali Pasha, was able to carve, by unscrupulous treachery and merciless cruelty, a private principality centred on Epirus, where he was visited by Lord Byron. After forty years he was finally reduced by the Turks, but not before the Greek War of Independence had started in 1821.

On the 25th of March, the feast of the Annunciation, the Archbishop of Patras proclaimed Greek independence at the Monastery of Aghia Lavra in the Peloponnese. The Turks retaliated with the massacres of Greeks on Chios, in Macedonia and Constantinople, where the Patriarch was hanged on Easter Sunday.

The heroic expoits of the Greeks inspired numerous Philhellenic volunteers, especially British, among them Lord Byron who died in Messolonghi. The intervention by an Egyptian army and fleet in support of the Turks led in 1825 to the formation of a Triple Alliance of Great Britain, France and Russia, whose navy decisively defeated the Turco-Egyptian force at Navarino two years later.

The Protocol of London in 1832 established the frontier of the reborn Greek state, first a republic under the Corfiote nobleman Capo d'Istria, who had for a time been the Czar's foreign minister, and after his murder as a kingdom under the young Bavarian Prince, Otho. After a bloodless revolution in 1843, which culminated in the proclamation of a liberal constitution, Otho was forced to abdicate in 1863.

An overwhelming majority voted to offer the vacant throne to Queen Victoria's second son, the Duke of Edinburgh. But the dynasties of the three Protecting Powers were excluded, and the acceptance of their joint choice, Prince George of Denmark, was made popular by the cession of the Ionian Islands by Great Britain to Greece. In 1881 Thessaly was incorporated in the Kingdom of the Hellenes, but the Cretan uprising in 1897 led to an unseccessful war with Turkey and in the following year to the granting of full autonomy to Crete under purely nominal Turkish suzerainty.

The two Balkan Wars of 1912 and 1913 almost doubled Greece's territory and population, but in the interval King George I was murdered in the newly conquered Thessaloniki. His son and heir, King Konstantine lacked his father's political foresight; having received his military training in Germany he believed in the final victory of the German Emperor William II, whose sister he had married. The Allies intervened and forced

King Konstantine to leave the country where his second son, Alexander, became king.

In 1920 he died of blood-poisoning from a monkey bite, and by another of the many plebiscites King Konstantine was recalled. After a disastrous war with the resurgent Turks in Asia Minor, in defence of the vast gains made by the Treaty of Sèvres, Greece had to resign itself to the frontier of the Evros river in Thrace and an unprecedented exchange of populations, 1,500.000 Greeks against 370.000 Turks, which burdened the small country tremendous social and economic problems. Kind Konstantine abdicated now in favour of his eldest son, who briefly ruled as George II before the proclamation of a republic in 1924. But the King was recalled by another plebiscite in 1935, only to leave the country again in 1941 after a heroic resistance against the Italians and Germans.

Returning as the result of the plebiscite of 1946, in the lull between two Communist rebellions, George II died the following year, before the end of the Civil War in 1949 in the reign of his brother, King Paul, who was succeed in 1964 by his son, King Konstantine.

Continual cabinet crises led to the military Revolution of the 21st April 1967 and in December of the same year the King left the country.

The military regime in Athens resigned July 23, 1974. Former Premier Caramanlis returned to Athens and was sworn in as Premier of Greece's first civilian government since 1967.

So long and varied a history naturally left splendid architectural and artistic remains scattered all over the country.

ATHENS AND ATTICA

It is called the violet-crowned, because just before sunset Mount Hymettus glows with a particularly soft purple-shaded light, which is reflected on the vast sprawling city below, in the unrivalled clearness of the Attic atmosphere.
the Attic atmosphere.

According to legend the Phoenician Kekrops founded the city on the rock of the Acropolis, whose patronage was disputed by two mighty Olympian gods, Poseidon and Athena. The council of gods would award the prize for the most useful gift; the god of the sea struck the rock with his trident and a splendid steed sprang forth, symbol of manly qualities; but the goddess of wisdom produced an olivetree, and this symbol of peace and prosperity assured her of the coveted town to be called after her, Athens.

Erechtheus, half-man, half-serpent, was buried in the oldest sanctuary, but with his successor Aegeus historical facts become part of the legend, the connection with the Minoan empire to which a blood tribute of seven youths and maidens had to be paid, in which Theseus, the king's son,, was included. His slaying of the Minotaur is the poetic expression of the overthrow of the Minoans by mainland Greeks. On his return Theseus forgot to change the black sails and his father, believing his son dead, plunged into the sea to which he gave his name, the Aegean.

Theseus united Attica, but it was only in the sixth century B.C. that Athens became a leading power, largely due to the wise rule of the Tyrant Peisistratus. He started the conversion of the Acropolis from a fortress into a sacred rocks by building several temples, which were destroyed by the Persians during their occupation of Athens in 480 B.C.

Themistocles started the refortification, but it was in the Golden Age of Pericles, that the Parthenon and Erechtheion, respectively the loveliest Dorian and Ionian temple were erected, together with the magnificent entrance of the propylaea and the temples at Sounion and Eleusis. Callicrates, Ictinus and Mnesicles were the architects who made Athens the wonder of antiquity with the assistance of the superb statuary of Pheidias and Myron. Even after the disastrous Peloponnesian War, the Athenians were able to complete the vast Theatre of Dionysus and the Stadium which, reconstructed, was the scene of the first modern Olympic Games in 1896.

Hellenistic kings vied with each other to embellish the town, but it was the Roman Emperor Hadrian who, next to Pericles, contributed the greatest architectural treasures. He finished the Temple of Olympian Zeus, built a Library, a new Market, while his graceful Arch indicates that a whole new town had sprung up. His friend, the immensely wealthy banker Herodes Atticus, built the Odeon in which the Athens Festival is now held each summer, clothed the Stadium in marble, and scattered his dedications to the greater beauty of the town he loved.

But in the following century decay set in, aggravated by the rise of Christianity in the fourth century, at the end of which Athens was sacked and ravaged by the Goths of Alaric.

Hence it decayed into insignificance, slightly relieved by the establishment of a Frankish principality in the thirteenth century, which brought incongruous medieval customs to the most classical of sites, and converted the ancient temples from the Orthodox to the Roman Catholic faith, so that the Holy Virgin was worshipped in the place of Athena.

The Turks came in 1445 and their commanders installed themselves in the Propylaea and their harem in the Erechtheion. The Parthenon was used as a gunpowder magazine and, hit by a shell dirung the Venetian siege of 1687, badly damaged.

Suffering further during the War of Independence, Athen was a village of some five thousand povertystricken inhabitants, when it was chosen as the capital of the kingdom in 1834. Today with the port of Piraeus and the outlying suburbs, it is a sprawling modern metropolis bursting with a population of over 3,500.000.

THE PELOPONNESE. Nowhere in Europe has prehistory been so impressively preserved as in Isle of Pelops, whose tragic family include Agamemnon, Klytemnestra, Menalaus, Helen of Troy, Orestes and Electra, to whose sinister destiny the ruins of Myceanae provide the fitting setting. Even more impressive are the Cyclopean ramparts of Tiryns, birthplace of Heracles.

Of the states established in the eleventh century B.C., the most powerful, Sparta, left the least architectural traces, as the Spartans always prided themselves on their simplicity. Of Dorian Corinth little but the sixth-century B.C. Temple of Apollo remains, as it was destroyed by the Romans in 146 B.C. and only rebuilt some hundred years later by order of Julius Caesar. The extensive ruins thus belong to the Roman period.

The splendid Theatre of Epidaurus, scene of another festival, and the sanctuarry of Asclepius, the god of healing, but above all Olympia, with its temples and treasuries, are among the most important remains of the classical Greek period, despite subsequent Hellenistic and Roman additions.

The Byzantines built the mighty fortresses of Acro-Corinth Monemvasia and Mistra; the last contains some particularly fine frescoes in its churches below the great Palace of the Despots. The Franks fortified their conquests by the strong castles of Tornese and Karytaena; the Venetians by Methoni, an outstanding example of medieval military architecture, Pylos and, leveliest of all, Nafplion, on its crag above modern Greece's first capital.

CENTRAL GREECE. The two outstanding sites could not be more different and yet are equally impressive. Delphi, antiquity's most celebrated oracle, rises dramatically on terrace beyond terrace below the towering rocks of Mount Parnassos. Its museum contains the finds from the temples, treasuries, theatre and stadium, from which the view extends over the Sea of Olives, a delicate silvery green, to the distant blue sea.

Meteora is purely medieval, an unearthly forest of gigantic rockneedles rising to 1,820 feet, five still crowned by Byzantine monasteries, once the retreat of kings and emperors.

THE ISLANDS. A world in itself, of unbelievable richness in natural and artistic beauty. Crete, in whose sumptuous palaces European civilisation achieved a first flowering. Delos, the wholy island of antiquity, where for a thousand years faith worshipped ever stranger gods. Thira (Santorini), an exploded volcano into which the ships sail past the still active remnants, one of the wonders of nature further enhanced by the recent discovery of a Minoan town. Rhodes and Kos, blending extensive Hellenistic remains into the great fortifications of the medieval Knights. The subtle veriety in the dazzling white churches and houses of Mykonos and Paros.
And in the Ionian Sea, Corfu, where the Venetians fitted the town so perfectly into the luxuriant vegetation.

EPIRUS AND MACEDONIA. Here some of the most interesting towns are located. Yannina, dominated by the minarets of Turkish mosques has retained much of the oriental atmosphere. Among the sea of modern houses of Thessaloniki hide some superb Byzantine churches, architectural jewels of the Middle Ages.

MOUNT ATHOS. On this Holy Mountain, the Chalkidiki's westernmost promontory, monks have lived for a thousand years organised into an independent theocratic republic, ever since the Emperor Nicephorus Phocas founded the *Monastery of Aghia Lavra* in 963, on the advice of Saint Athanasius, whose strict rules were adopted in all the Twenty Monasteries.

The Acropolis

THE ACROPOLIS

The Acropolis or (high city) is a rocky hill 156 m. above sea level, dominating the centre of the town. It is a true natural fortress since it is inaccessible from all sides except the west side where the entrance is located.

From the earliest times it had been both a fortress and the religious centre of the state. The principal cult was that of the goddess Athena and in her honour were constracted on the Acropolis splendid temples.

The most remarkable monuments: the Parthenon, the Erechtheion, the Propylaea, and the temple of Nike were built in the last half of the 5th century B.C. under the inspiration of Pericles and even in ruins witness «the glory that was Greece».

Aerial view of the Acropolis with the Mt. Lycabettus in the background

THE PROPYLAEA

The monumental gate was conceived and executed by the architect Mnesicles as «the radiant diadem of the citadel of the gods» between 437 and 432 B.C. Never quite completed because of the outbreak of the Peloponnesian War, the only opening in the encircling walls extends over 150 feet divided into a central portico and two asymmetrical wings, in two shades of marble and two orders of architecture, Doric outside and Ionian within.

On the right of the propylaea stands on a high platform a graceful little temple with eight Ionic columns, the temple of Athena Nike (Wingless Victory) built in the 5th century B.C. to commemorate the Greek victories over the Persians.

The Temple of Wingless victory (Nike).

The Propylaea seen from the Areopagus

Pericles addressing the Athenians on the hill of Pnyx.

Caryatids on the Erechtheion.

THE CARYATIDES

The most interesting part of the Erechtheion is the south Portico of the Caryatides or Maidens. Six statues of beautiful girls of outstanding craftsmanship. The colonnade exudes flexibility and charm. The figures stand four in front and two behind and they support an entablature like columns. The capitals of their heads are designed like baskets. Each rests her weight on the leg farthest from the center of the façade, and all produce the impression of ease and stability. The second Caryatid of the colonnade facing west is a copy plaster. The original was taken by Lord Elgin to London in 1801.

The name caryatides given to these figures in later times was derived from the town of Caryae, in Laconia.

THE ERECHTHEION

In this area are found the oldest and most sacred relics of ancient Athens, the mycenean palace, the tomb and shrine of Kekrops, the marks of Poseidon's trident, the sacred olive tree of Athena.

All these contributed and so the building has such a complicated plan. It was built between 421 and 406 B.C.

The basic plan is a rectangle with three porches in different levels. So in the interior we have two sanctuaries, one dedicated to Poseidon Erechtheus which was entered from the N. and one dedicated to Athena Polias which was entered from the E. The S. porch has six statues of Korai-(maidens). It is an ionic edifice with rich and elegant decoration and perfect elaboration of sur faces.

The Erechtheion.

The Odeum of Herodes Atticus during the Athens Festival.

The Athens Festival of Music and Drama is held every summer with the participation of the world's greatest conductors, soloists, orchestras, theatre and ballet companies in the Theatre of Herodes Atticus. The Greek Royal Theatre presents ancient tragedies and commedies, which are also performed in the Lycabettus Theatre, while the Philopappus Theatre is given over to folk dancing.

The «Sound and Light» performances on the Pnyx highlight the great moments in the history of the Acropolis.

The Acropolis illuminated.

THE PARTHENON

The Parthenon, built on the highest part of the Acropolis, is the most important creation of ancient Greek architecture and a symbol of the perfection that marked the classical spirit of the age of Pericles — 5th century B.C. — the «Golden Age» of Greek history. It was built during the period 447-438 B.C. by the architects Ictinus and Callicrates. The composition and sculpture of its ornamentations were the work of the great Phidias, who was also the co-ordinator of the whole plan.

An eternal symbol of aesthetic perfection, this temple was dedicated to the goddess Athena, the Patroness of Athens. Of Doric order, the temple was made of marble extracted from Mt. Pendeli. Its length is 69.51 m. and its width 30.87 m. Although partly ruined today — largely due to the bombardment by Morozini in 1687 — it still fills the visitor with admiration and awe.

THE ACROPOLIS MUSEUM

In the Acropolis Museum are exhibited sculptures and other finds from the Acropolis. At the present moment the Museum consists of IX Rooms. The Visitor may see sculptures of the archaic period (6th cent), the classical period and a few of Hellenistic and Roman periods.

The «Mourning Athena»

Acropolis Museum Gods: Poseidon, Apollo, Artemis.

The Theatre of Dionysius.

THE THEATRE OF DIONYSUS

The Theatre of Dionysus (southern slope of the Acropolis). As early as the 6th century the official Athenian theatre was on this site, forming part of the great sanctuary of Dionysus, during whose festival plays were performed. It was here that the works of Aescylus, Sophocles, Euripides and Aristophanes were first performed, though much of the stone work of the extant building actually dates from the start of the 4th C.B.C. Apart from its artistic function, it was also used for public meetings.

ODEON OF HERODES ATTICUS

It was built in 161 A. D. by Herodes Atticus in memory of his wife Regilla and served as a theatre and concert hall. It has 32 rows of seats which can hold 5.000 spectators.
According to Philostratos the Odeon was covered with a wooden roof.

The Odeum of Herodes Atticus

The Stoa of Attalus.

The Ceramic Cemetery

CERAMICOS

In Ceramicos, the ill‖
strious Athenian we‖
buried by the stat‖
particularly those wh‖
had fallen in batt‖
Their tombs were m‖
de on either side ‖
great road leading ‖
Academy.

THE TEMPLE OF HEPHAESTUS

The Theseum (correctly called the Hephaisteum as it was consecrated to the god Hephaistos) is the most intact of all the known Greek temples. A mixture of Doric and Ionic elements, it is probably slightly older than the Parthenon. It stands on a slight rise overlooking the extensive remain of the ancient market-place (agora) at the north-west foot of the acropolis, and facing the restored Roman stoa of Attalos.

The temple of Hephaistus (Theseion).

The Bema in the Pnyx.

THE PNYX

From this rostrum cut into the rock the orators Solon, Pericles and Demosthenes — but also a much larger number of demagogues harangued the Athenians in the first attempt at direct democracy.

THE MONUMENT OF PHILOPAPPUS

The highest hill (481 feet) facing the Acropolis is crowned by the ruined marble monument of Philopappus, a Syrian prince and Roman consul, honoured by the Athenians in 116 A.-D. for his gifts to their city.

The Monument of Philopappos.

TOWER OF WINDS

The Tower of the winds.

The 1st century B.C. Tower of the Winds was a gift of Andronicus Cyrrhestes, a hydraulic clock with a sun dial and weather vane.
The form of the marble octagon corresponds to the eight winds, whose symbolic winged figures are represented on the frieze.

The Temple of the Olympian Zeus.

THE TEMPLE OF ZEUS

Hadrian completed the temple of Olympian Zeus about 700 years after Peisistratus had raised the first immense columns — 7 feet 10 inches in diameter. The 104 Corinthian marble columnus of the Roman sanctuary were a third smaller, though still the largest in Europe, as was the temple itself, 354 by 135 feet. The Roman general Sulla removed the pillars of the intervening Hellenistic temple to Rome in the first century B.C.; Genoese and Venetians did likewise with Hadrian's marbles, so that only 16 columns now remain 13 standing together under their architraves.

The Arch of Hadrian.

THE ARCH OF HADRIAN

The slender arch consisting of an apsis decorated with Corinthian columns proclaims on the western side «This is the city of Theseus» and on the eastern «This is the city of Hadrian». Hadrian indeed greatly enlarged the town and established entire new quarters north of the temple of Zeus.

Bronze statue of Poseidon (or Zeus) 460 Cent. B.C.

GREEK ARCHAEOLOGICAL TREASURE
IN THE MUSEUMS

Close to all the main classical sites are museu
containing the priceless heritage of the plastic
that has been saved from Greece's great p
sculpture, temple triezes, trescoes, pottery and j
lery of all ages, from the angular and quasi abs
decorations on the vases of the geometric pe
through to the overripe curves and lush rea
of Hellenistic and Greco-Roman statuary. By fa
biggest and most dazzling collections is in the N
nal Archaeological Museum in Athens (Odo
Okto vriou). Most famous are the Mycenaean
work including the death mask of Agamemnon
strange archaic figures from the Cyclades that
to mind the techniques of modern sculpture,
preclassical kouroi (youths), and the sculptur
the golden age, famous for its nobility and perf
on of line, as in the Youth of Anticythera or
bronze statue of Zeus.

Gold Mask of Mycenae.

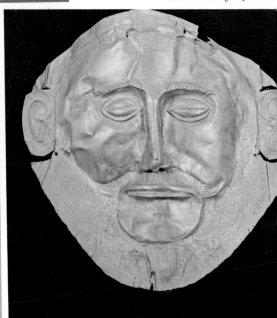

Bronze race horse with its small Jockey. Found in 1927 of Cape Artemision in Euboea together with the bronze statue of Poseidon. About the middle of the 2nd century B.C.

The Panathenaic Stadium.

Evzones of the Presidential gua[rd]

MODERN ATHEMS

A view across the modern city of Athens towards Mount Lycavettos. This hill, which according to legend was thrown down by Athena when she learnt of the disobedience of the daughters of Cecrops, dominates, the town, with a panoramic view across the Piraeus to the Saronic Gulf. On the summit of the hill is the Chapel of St. George.

Part of Central Athens with Mt. Lycavitos in the background.

The picturesque Mikrolimano (Tourkolimano).

THE PIRAEUS

A corner of the harbour at the Piraeus. The father of the Athenian navy, Themistocles, initiated the task of founding a port here at the outset of the fifth century B.C. and the construction of the famous Long Walls running down from Athens to the sea (by Kimon and Pericles) copleted his object. It at once became a cosmopolitan commercial centre, a character which the modern city has rapidly regained in the 20th century, adding to it the face of a highly developed industrial complex.

The port of Piraeus.

SOUNION

Sounion. The Temple of Poseidon.

The wind-swept cape was an obvious choice for a sanctuary of Poseidon, where the sailors might offer a last sacrifice to propitiate the mighty God of the Sea, before leaving the comparative safety of the Saronic Gulf for the perils of the open archipelago. The archaic temple was destroyed by the Persians in 480 B.C. and rebuilt like numerous other shrines throughout Attica by Pericles. The pure whiteness of the 12 remaining Doric columns is still as dazzling against the deep-blue sky as in the days of Byron who carved his name into the marble.

On a lower hill, beyond the fortifications of the Peloponnesian War, stands the temple of Athena Sounias, a simple rectangle to which Ionian colonnades were later added on two sides.

The Monastery of Kaissariani.

THE MONASTERY OF KAISSARIANI

Of the five monasteries on Mount Hymettus, the retreat of Kaissariani — though long disaffected — is by far the most romantic. Built on a sanctuary of Aphrodite near a spring, the 11th-century hexagonal cupola supported by four Ionian columns blends harmoniously with the later narthex and campanile. The 16th-century frescoes portray the Virgin seated between the Archangels in the apse and the Apostles on the north wall.

The refectory, kitchen and some cells have been restored in the charming setting of the wooded slopes.

DAPHNI

The Emperor Justinian constructed a fortified monastery over the ruined temple of Apollo, but the church of the Assumption with its magnificent mosaics was only added some 500 years later.

The Frankish dukes invited Cistercian monks as guardians of their last resting place and two sarcophagi with fleurs-de-lis still stand in the Gothic cloisters.

When the last duke strangled his aunt before Daphni's altar, Sultan Mohammed II occupied Athens executed the duke and expelled the Cistercians. After centuries of neglect Orthodox monks returned and defended the monastery during the War of Indepedence. Following extensive restorations the superb mosaic of Christ Pantocrator looks again severaly down on biblical scenes of astounding freedom of line and delicate colouring.

The Crist Mosaic in the Daphni.

Daphni.

THE CORINTH CANAL

The Corinth Canal, begun 1882 and completed 1893. The idea of cutting a canal through the narrow neck of the isthmus which joins the Peloponnese to the rest of Greece was conceived in classical times and seriously investiga ted by several Roman emperors. The present canal is 6,939 yards long, its bed width is 75,6 as at Suez, the depth of water is 26,3. It shortens the voyage between the Adriatic and the Piraeus by some 200 miles.

A panoramic view of Loutraki.

The Corinth Canal.

OLD CORINTH

The Temple of Apollo at Corinth, one of the oldest in Greece (epoch of Periander c. 585 B.C.). In classical times, Corinth was famous as a trading centre, and for its love of luxury and pleasures. Its maritime interest led it to its advantage into the anti-Athenian camp in the quarrels which reft Greece in the fourth century B.C. Above the site towers Acrocorinth where the famous sacred prosititudes once had their temple. An imposing fortress was later built there of which extensive ruins survive and was held successively by Byzantines, Franks, Venetians and Turks. In 1208, its last Byzantine commander, Leon Sgouros, met his doom by riding his horse over the precipitous edge rather than surrender to the Franks.

Mycenae. The Tomb of Klytemnistra.

MYCENAE

Mycenae inheritor of the Cretan Empire, looks out across the Plan of Argos to the sea. Its elevated position afforded protection from surprise attacks by pirates. At the time of its power (c. 1400 B.C.) the population was grouped around the vast central fortress where the reigning family had its residence and burial place. The famous Gate of the Lions is in the north-west corner of the fortress (the design is Cretan); the passage beyond it leads to the royal graveyard where Schliemann discovered priceless treasures in 1876. Outside the fortress proper lie the impressive beehive tombs including that ascribed to Agamemnon (above). The stone over the doorway alone is reckoned to weight some 120 tons. After the burial of the head of the family, the entrance passage was completely filled with earth to prevent the plundering of the tomb.

The Lions Gate, the main entrance to the Acropolis of Mycenae.

The ancient Theatre of Epidaurus.

EPIDAVROS

The ancient town of Epidavros, near the east coast of the Peloponnese, was famous as the most important centre for the worship of Aesculapius, the god of medecine. When a patient recovered after treatment by the doctor priests, he would dedicate a replica of the part of his anatomy that had been affected and the museum there contains a remarkable collection of these fascinating offerings. Within the sacred precincts were also included a stadium and a great theatre. This latter, the work of Polycleitos the Younger (late 4th century B.C.), is the best preserved of any edifice of this kind. Its seating capacity is approximately 15,000 and its acoustics are superb. A festival of ancient drama is performed there every summer by the Royal Theatre Company.

NAFPLION

The Burzi islet, close to the entrance of Nafplion harbour. This fort, buit by the Venetians, is now a hotel.
An aerial view of the Nafplion peninsula. The Acronafplion citadel which dominates the town from a height of 279 feet occupies the site of the ancient Acropolis whose foundations serve as a base for the Venetian and Turkish ramparts. Parts of the Venetian fortress were later employed as a prison.

Bourdzi, the old Venetian fortress at Nauplia.

About 20 miles from Gythion lies the vast and beautiful complex of the Dirou caves. In the largest, the river winds in a half mile loop through a series of chambers and corridors, decorated with the fantasy shapes of stalactites, stalagmites and water-sculptured pillars.

Mani. Dirou Caves. Vlychada.

MISTRAS

In 1248 the Frankish Prince of Achaia, Guillaume Villehardouin, having gained complete control of the south Peloponnese, decided to set up a fortress to control the area and chose one of the foothills of the Taygetos above the Plain of Sparta. The castle was called Mistra (Myzithra in mediaeval Greek) because the hill on which it stood resembled a cheese of that name. Ten years late Guillaume was captured in Macedonia fighting against the Byzantine emperor, Michael Paleologus, and the beautiful castle, the pride of his heart, was sacrificed as part of his ransome. A Greek general was installed and the hill was transformed into a Byzantine city with mansions, churches, and monasteries that still stand today. It flourished as an intellectual centre and was very dear to the Imperial family. In the cathedral of St. Demetrius, most important of all the churches of the city, the last Emperor of Byzantium, Constantine Palaiologue, was crowned in 1449. The city fought bittely on for 8 years after the fall of Constantinople in 1453, before capitualting to the Turks.

Mystra, the Church of «Pantanassa».

The Temple of Apollo Epikourios at Vassae.

The Temple of Vassae, one of the best preserved temples in Greece. Its slender columns rise in solitary splendour on a plateau amid the wild mountains. Dedicated to Apollo, it was probably erected between 420-417 B.C. by Ictinos, architect of the Parthenon. It was commissioned by the people of the town of Phygalia because they believed that Apollo had delivered them from a plague during the Peloponnesian War.

MONEMVASIA

Monemvasia (whose name means «having only one entrance») was originally almost an island, but the Byzantines strengthened its connection with the land by a causeway 164 yards long. It later passed into the hands of a succession of foreign conquerors. It is notable for its churches, Renaissance houses and fine Venetian fortifications.

METHONI

Methoni stands at the point of a promontory in the southwest Peloponnese. Along the sweep of its beautiful sandy bay runs a magnificent 13th century citadel, partly rebuilt by the Venetians in 514, and again by the French in 1828.

The rock island of Monemvasia.

Old fort at Methoni.

OLYMPIA

Olympia, in the western Peloponnese, lies in the peaceful pineclad valley of the River Alpheos. It gained its fame as a sanctuary of Zeus and Hera, but the site also contains a wealth of other small shrines, gymnasiums and sculptors' workshops. It was in the still extant stadium that the Olympic Games were founded, accordings to tradition, in 776 B.C., and the Greeks calculated their chronology from this date, measuring events by the Olympiad in which they occured. It is from here the sacred troch is still carried to whatever corner of the world the modern Olympiads are held in. The period of the Games was always marked by a Sacred Truce during which all the people of Greek race forgot their differences and united for a while in the spirit of Hellenism. In the Olympia Museum are exhibited unique sculptural masterpieces, such as Praxiteles' Hermes, Paeoneus' Victory, Apollo and many other art trasures.

Chalkis. The strait of Euripos with the modern Bridge.

THERMOPYLAE

Leonidas, King of Sparta, commanded the defence of the mainland at the pass of Thermopylae, making a heroic last stand with his three hundred Spartans who were, after betrayal, stain to the last man.

Thermopylae: The Statue of Leonidas, King of Sparta.

The Byzantine monastery of Ossios Loukas.

OSSIOS LOUKAS

in the 11th century A.D. in honour of a local saintly hermit who had prophesied his capture of Crete. The most interesting of its buildings is the main church, with its mosaics, rich furnishings and variegate marble floors. The mosaics are considered equal to those of Daphni and Constantinople.

The Bronze statue of the Charioteer

◄Delphi. The Tholos of Marmarias

DELPHI

Delphi. The temple of Apollo.

Delphi, was the religious centre of classical Greece. Backed by the huge crags of the Shining Rocks and looking down a wild gorge to the Gulf of Corinth, it is one of the most beautiful and awe inspiring sights in the world.

The ancient Greeks chose this unique spot for their most sacred and famed Oracle, that of Apollo, which influenced the fate of states and individuals alike for about 1000 years (7th cent. B.C. to 4th cent. A.D.), and was the greatest santcuary and spiritual centre of the world of that time. The crystalline waters of the sacred Castalia spring flow at the foot of the Phaedriades Rocks.

The sacred area also comprises an ancient theatre (3rd cent. B.C.), a Stadium and a Museum with numerous statues, among which is the masterly bronze statue of the Charioteer. It's dated c. 475 B.C.

Parga, a very pleasant little town on the coast of Epirus.

The Ancient Theatre at Dodona

DODONA. In a serenely peaceful vale, 12 km southwest of Yannina, lies Europe's oldest sanctuary, where oracles were interpreted from the rustling of the wind in the leaves of the sacred oak tree as far back as the third millenium B.C.

The oracle was consulted by Achilles, Heracles and other mythological heroes, manking in importance second only to Delphi. The Macedonian kings particularly favoured Dodona which they adorned with temples, porticoes and one of the largest Theatres in Greece, restored for the annual Summer Festival of Ancient Drama.

Ioannina. The perama cave.

Yannina, capital of the Epirus and fourth city of modern Greece, stands on a legendary lake in whose waters are mirrored the imposing Castro (Citadel) on its rock and the Aslan Aga mosque beneath which, following a barbarous custom, seventeen women were put to death in 1801. It was a cultural and commercial centre even under the Turks, especially renowned for its gold and silver smiths. At the turn of the eighteenth century the notorious Ali Pasha made so powerful that the Sultan was obliged to move against him to reestablish central authority in 1822. It was Ali's mistress, the Lady Phrosyne who met her death in the waters of the lake. Close to Yannina is the Perama cave, famous, for its beautiful stalactites.

Ioannina the picturesque Lakeside.

The village of Makrynitsa on Mt. Pelion.

THE "METEORA"

Near the small town of Kalambaka in Thessaly a number of gigantic vertical rocks tower majestically over the plain. Their strange shapes and bare majesty make them one of the most beautiful and fantastic landscapes in Greece. On the tops of these rocks - average altitude 300 m. - pious monks set up monasteries in the 15th and 16th centuries A.D. and called them "Meteora", to imply (the Greek meaning of the world) "suspended between sky and earth". Of the 24 monasteries on the summits, only 4 are inhabited to-day, namely the Great Meteoron - the Varlaam monastery - Agios Stefanos monastery - Aghia Trias monastery. Everyone who visits the "Meteora" leaves the place with an unforgettable impression of rare natural beauty. The visitor also has the opportunity of admiring the old artistic wall paintings, icons, and rare old manuscripts, all of which are of great historical significance as well as being gems of Byzantine art.

The Monastery of Aghia Triada.

EDESSA

Edessa (Macedonia) perched over 1000 ft. above sea level commands an exquisite view of the northern plains. Criss-crossing it are the streams the unite to form the famous falls. The water tumples 82 ft., between cliffs covered with a riot of rich vegetation, vines figs, pome- granate and walnut trees.

CASTORIA

Casto.ia stands on a promontory that juts out into the beautiful Lake Orestias. Built on the ruins of the city founded by Justinian in the 6th c. A.D., it is a colourful town containing many old aristocratic mansions, richly painted and ornamented with fine carved woodwork. There are also 72 very old churches, of which the Panayia Kouveliotissa is one a charming little church, of triconic plan, decorated in square around the dome.

The inhabitants of the town, where a fur industry flourishes, are noted for their hospitality

The Waterfalls

at Edessa.

Tempe:
Pinios river.

Kastoria. Orestias Lake.

Mt. Olympus

MOUNT OLYMPUS. The Th[rone] of Zeus, where the anti[ent] world placed the palaces of [the] Twelve Olympian Gods, actua[lly] is only the third highest amo[ng] the majestic peaks, which r[ise] over 3.000 m in a semicir[cle] above the remote Mavrolong[o] Valley. The highest, Mytikas [or] The Needle, was only climbe[d in] 1913, as a superstitious a[we] remained attached to this mig[h]ty range long after the old r[eli]gion had fallen.

PELLA

Capital of ancient Maced[o]nia, seat of both Phillip [II] and his son, Alexander t[he] Great. Ruins of the city. Fi[ne] mosaics in the Museum.

Pella. The ruins.

Thessaloniki The White Tower.

THESSALONIKI

Thessaloniki, the lively modern city overlooking the lovely Gulf of Thermai is the capital of Macedonia and second city of Greece today. St. Paul preached here, and the wealth of 14th c. Byzantine churches testifies to the heights to which Cristianity then attained in the city. Along the sea promenade the White Tower, last remainder of the 15th c. fortifications has become Thessalonikis unofficial emblem. Close to it, an International Trade Fair is held every September which is one of the most important industrial events in the Eastern Mediterranean.

Thassos. The most thickly wooded Greek island.

PHILIPPI

Philippi. Named after the town which took its name from Philip II in 356 B.C. The city became widely known after the battle fought there by two Roman armies in 42 B.C. This battle resulted in the crowning of Octavius Augustus as the first Roman Emperor. Today the visitor can see the remains of the Agora with its public buildings the sacred gates, public baths, wresting rings and the theatre, where ancient dramas are now poerormed. It was here, too, that the Apostle Paul gave his first sernon of the new faith.

A view of Kavala and its harbour.

remains at the Archeological site of Philippi.

Chalkidiki. Picturesque view of Marmara.

CHALKIDIKI

Of all the many beautiful and vari landscapes of Greece, Chalkidiki itself an instance of contrast a variety, idyllic and rugged by turns panorama of mountain and sea tha enticing and fascinating to explor A world in itself, as yet unravaged the cohorts of modern tourism, Cha diki offers the ultimum in holidaymakin a wealth of natural beauties, t vestiges of a proud and tumultuo past, the 1000-yet old Byzantine tre sures of the Holy Mountain of Atho and all those sophisticated attractio of top-ranking tourist resorts whi make for a thoroughly pleasurable a rewarding holiday.

CHALKIDIKI
Ouranoupolis.

MOUNT ATHOS

Located on a headland on the easternmost of the Chalkidiki peninsula in Macedonia, Mount Athos (Holy Mountain) constitutes the only entirely monastic state in Europe. Its 20 fortress-like monasteries and countless hermitages scattered over rugged and dramatic countryside contain many rare objects of Byzantine art and priceless manuscripts. No women or youths under 21 (except theological students) are allowed to go there.

Mount Athos. The Monastery of Saint Panteleimon.

Mount Athos. The monastery of Grigoriou

THE GREEK ISLANDS

Whatever direction you take across the Aegean, there is always some island rising across the horizon. Whether wild and green, like the northern islands (Thasos and the N. Sporades), stark and sheer like the southern islands (the Cyclades), or cultivatedly luxuriant like the eastern group (Mytilene, Chios, Samos), they all have the same air of suspended time, the same little whitewashed churches, the same pack-donkeys pacing the cobbled streets, the same fishing boats placidly riding in the harbour with great eyes painted on their prows just as they were thousands of years ago. Apart from the groups already mentioned, to the south-east is the Dodecanese, a rope of twelve islands strung against the Turkish coast, with Rhodes, the largest and most lustrous, for its clasp. Farther south still is the greatest and most complex of all the islands, Grete, a microcosm of the whole range of Greek scenery, inhabited by a fiercely independent people, almost a race apart. Everywhere one is reminded of the richness of the past by ancient cities and temples, mediaeval castles, Byzantine monasteries. For those who want a gay social life, there are bright, busy islands like Mykonos (Cyclades) and Hydra (Saronic Gulf), for those who want to withdraw into nature and forget the existence of the rest of the world, there are isolated, peaceful islands like Ios (Cyclades). Nor must we forget the western islands, the Ionian group headed by Corfu, with their more Adriatic beauty, and that strange legacy of English rule, the only regular cricket team in the whole Mediterranean. Whichever island you choose, one thing is certain. You will everywhere be dazzled by the same penetrating light and turquoise sea which have made their beauty legendary.

Aegina: The Temple of Aphaia (5th century B.C.).

THE TEMPLE OF APHAIA

The splendid Doric *Temple of Aphaia* dominates the east coast of the island of Aegina from a platform surrounded by pine trees. Aphaia was a local goddess, probably of Minoan provenance, but because the statue of Athena was so promunently displayed it was long assumed that the sanctuary was dedicated to her. In fact it was a memorial commemorating the great victory at Salamis, the pediments portraying earlier Greek successes over the Trojans, with Athena lending a helping hand. This sculpture of Parian marble was purchased in 1813 by Crown Prince Louis of Bavaria, father of modern Greece's first king.

Below the Temple is the popular beach of Aghia Marina.

Poros, pictturesque little island in the Saronic Gulf.

Hydra with its austerely beautiful old mansions and its picturesque little haven for Caiques and yachts.

Myconos, island of windmills.

MYCONOS

Myconos, one of the most popular tourist resorts, is a small bare island from where caiques cross to Delos (1/2 hr. trip.) It is famous for its many windmills and its 365 churches and chapels, many of which were dedicated by shipwrecked sailors. There are several good beaches, and in the summer nightlife is very lively.

Lions of the Naxians in Delos.

DELOS

Delos, the hub of the circle from which the Cyclades take their name. This tiny island, now deserted, was the most sacred in ancient Greece and honoured as the birthplace of Apollo and his sister Artemis. The ruins of the shrines and the great commercial centre that grew up around them cover the island. The famous marble lions an offering by the island of Naxos, line the Sacred Way leading to the main temples.

The island of Ios in the Cyclades.

The Aegean island of Paro

SANTORINI

Santorini (or Thira) is one of the most interesting islands of the Cyclades. It is visited by numberless foreigners and Greeks every summer, who flock there to admire the extraordinary landscapes that have been created by its volcano and by earthquakes.

On the island there flourished a local civilization dating back to prehistoric times. The ruins of that civilization are buried under thick blankets of lava. Excavations have unearthed quite a few

Santorini. View of the capital. Phera.

THE N. SPORADES

Skiros, Skopelos, Skiathos and Alonissos form a little archipelago to the north of Euboea. Both Skopelos and Skiathos are very verdant, and the latter is essentially a fisherman's island, with a charming sheltered port and a tradition of boat building. The bay at Koukounaries which takes its name from the sweet-scented pines that fringe its sweeping golden sands, is one of the most beautiful natural beaches in the whole Mediterranean.

Koukounaries at Skiathos.

Ithaca, the island Kingdom of Odysseus.

Zakynthos (Zante) The church of Aghios Dionysios

THE IONIAN ISLANDS

To the west of Greece lie the Ionian islands, also known as the Heptanese because there are seven main islands in the group. Not only geographically but also historically they form a bridge between Greece and Italy, since during the 14c. and 15.c in face of the Turkish threat they voluntarily surrendered their sovereignity to Venice, three centuries of whose rule left a considerable stamp on the language and traditions of the area. The four chief islands, Corfu (ancien Corcyra), Lefkas, Zakynthos and Ithaca (home of Odysseus) are noted for their mountainous and verdant Adriatic beauty.

Assos, one of the most lovely spots in Cephalonia.

Corfu. Achilleion, the statue of Achilles

Corfu. Pontikonissi island and Vlacherna Monastery in foreground.

DODECANESE

The name "/Dodecanese'" means "Twelve islands", (there are actually thirteen). The best-known of these are Rhodes,Kos, and Patmos, famous all for their natural beauty and for their classical and mediaeval monuments. Kos was the home of Hippocrates, father of European medicine, and legend has it that the great plane tree still growing near the mosque is the very one under which he sat to dispence his medical advise. Patmos is renowned as the place to which in 95 A.D. St. John the Divine was banished, and where he wrote the Book of Revelations. The monastery there contains many valuable possessions. Attractive among the smaller islands is Symi lying in a bay of the Turkish coast. In its port there is a Byzantine castle and a church with frescoes. But the main island of the group is of course Rhodes, famous in classical times for the Colossus, one of the seven wonders of the ancient world which bestrode the entrance to its harbour. The deer, poised on their narrow columns, have become the emblems of the island since mediaeval times. Aside from the town of Rhodes itself with its turkish and mediaeval flavour,there are exquisite classical ruins at Kamiros and Lindos.

Lindos. The bay and the Acropolis.

Lindos. Doric temple which was dedicated to Athena.

KOS

The Hellenistic Asclepeion, famed medical centre in the island of Kos, has been partly reconstructed on three artificial terraces above the therapeutic springs. On the highest level stands a *Doric Temple*, on the middle terrace rises the *Great Altar of Asclepios*, flanked by two temples, while a *Stoa* and *Baths* occupied the lower. Nearby was the school building where the teachings of Hippocrates were handed down. From the "Spring of Hippocrates higher up the mountainside water still flows to the town.

Kos. Sanctuary of Asklepios, god of Medicine.

Patmos. The monastery of Saint John.

View of Symi.

KNOSSOS

Knossos is a picturesque spot near Heraklion, Crete. A town flourished there in very ancient times (3rd-1st millenium B.C.) and it was the kingdom of Minos, the prehistoric ruler of the seas. It was the first spark of European civilization, the Minoan.

Today the visitor will see the restored ruins of Minos' palace, unearthed in 1900 by the British archaeologist Evans.

The many - storeyed palace was the centre of a big tree-surrounded town without protective walls.

Built in the 19th Century B.C. it was destroyed by earthquake and rebuilt in the 17th Century B.C.

Its complex architecture, its lordly chambers and staircases, its perfect baths with their drainage system, its masterly wall paintings, statuettes, precious jewels and carved vases, all compel the visitor's admiration.

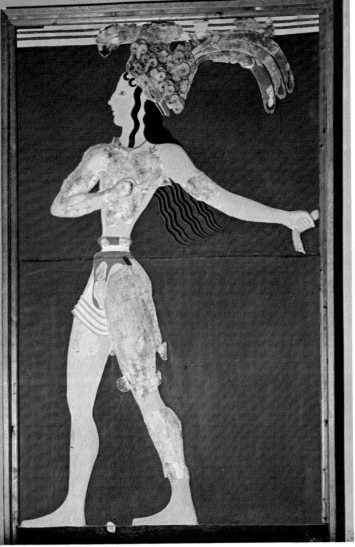

Knossos palace. The Prince with the Lilies.

The Prince with the lilies, also known the Priest — king, is one of the bas-relief frescoes in the palace of Minos at Knossos. It shows the typical portrait of a Cretan noble, bare-chested and muscular, but wasp - waisted and with long black curly hair.

Crete. The western Bastion of North Entrance Palace of Knossos.

CRETE

The island is a miniature of Greece itself in the complexity of its character. Geographically it varied from the wild, wooded mountains of western Crete to the long, fertile stretches of the central and coastal plains which are backed by the savage, soaring peaks of the range which includes Mount Ida. Along both the south and north coasts, there are winding beaches of white sand where sometimes long lines of surf curl in, and at the easternmost tip the shore is fringed with groves of date palms. As for antiquities, they abound from all epochs. Aside from the central palace at Knossos there is a very lovely palace further east along the coast at Mallia. Here the quite undefended position of the site, which runs on to the beach, reveals the confidence of the Cretan Empire in its own naval supremacy. There are also palaces at Phaistos and nearby at Aghia Triada on the south coast, and another has just been discovered at Zakros in the east. Both the capital, Heraklion, and Chanea in western Crete, the second largest town, have a mediaeval air, the former with its Venetian fortifications and fountain in the main square, the latter with its tall Venetian houses and harbour fort. And there are innumerable Byzantine churches like the interesting fortified twelfth century monastery of Toplou near Sitia in eastern Crete. The visitor too will be impressed with modern Crete and its independence. The island has its own rich folklore, its own music and dances, its own crafts. Fabrics are still woven in original Cretan patterns and colours, and particularly in the mountain villages many of the men still wear Cretan dress, with the distinctive black fringed kerchief bound around their foreheads. The island prides itslf too on itself contribution to modern Greek culture including among its sons the painter El Greco and the novelist and philosopher Kazantsakis.

Grete. The famous Gorge of Samaria

Crete. Dancers with National costumes.

Crete. the picturesque town of Aghios Nikolas.

Idyllic coast in Saronic Gulf.